Reignite Your Joy: Let God Lead Your Dance Through Life

DAR GEIGER

FOREWORD

As I started reading *Reignite Your Joy* by Dar Geiger, I began writing down golden nuggets, lessons learned and ideas I wanted to share with others. I found myself highlighting nearly every page, chuckling out loud at many parts and even crying while smiling as I read Dar's transformational journey, miraculous breakthroughs and a life of sorrow, addictions and loneliness turned completely around. Indeed, sometimes life has to turn you upside down before it can turn you right side up.

When I finished the book, my heart was full, and I found myself smiling and believing in miracles even more.

Dar hired me as a Transformational Coach after watching an interview I did for the Wake Up with Giants TV Facebook page.

At our first session, she shared with me her greatest desire was to empower and inspire women to embrace laughter, be brave, rise strong after setbacks, learn to live the second half of life better than the first and find what makes life truly beautiful after life's storms.

After our 6 weeks of coaching, I saw a book bubbling up inside of Dar and a doorway for her to help equip women to turn tears and hopelessness to passion, purpose and JOY. I found myself smiling a lot more after reading the insights from Dar. I found those smiles would turn to chuckles, then belly laughs bubbling out like a ray of sunshine, resulting in deeper wisdom and greater love for life and God.

I believe every person must go through sorrow and set back to understand compassion, empathy and to fully embrace joy in Christ. Not every person knows how to be happy and joyful and find God in the mess of life. Dar knows how and teaches the messages in authenticity through her life experiences. In her book, *Reignite Your Joy*, the reader will learn how to overcome trials and see life as a treasure hunt of miracles rather than a dead-end or a life of drudgery.

Dar spent much of the first half of her life running from God and the second half running after Him. She shares her golden formula on how she went from being a victim, experiencing loneliness and a life of struggles to abundant living and loving self and others.

Those that cross her path and learn the lessons she teaches will never be the same.

Dar beautifully teaches the power of forgiveness, surrendering, how to be resilient, love deep, navigate addictions with strength, and how to allow God to fill in the blanks.

Reignite Your Joy provides guidance to life's really tough experiences, and that there really is joy available. It also reminds us that when we are at our lowest, Christ stands ready to comfort and restore us.

I feel humbled and awed as I witness the transformation journey of Dar, and feel everyone needs to read this book – a true offer of love.

Dr. Rachel Smartt N.D.
Transformational Coach, Speaker, League of Giants
CEO of Smartt Transformations
Author of **Modern Day Miracles**

DAR GEIGER

DEDICATION

I dedicate this book to Jesus Christ, Lord and Savior of the world...

...and, to those who are seeking joy and stability.

DAR GEIGER

CONTENTS

INTRODUCTION

Do you remember your very first dance with a partner? Maybe you were invited to your high school prom by someone who was smitten with you in class. Maybe you attended a dance with friends, and someone you did not even think knew you existed asked you to dance. My first memory is dancing on daddy's feet while he took steps to the beat of a song on the radio. No matter when your first dance took place, my bet is that you remember the event with a smile.

How will you remember the year 2020? COVID-19, school closures, job loss, shortage of supplies, unexpected loss of life and fear of what the future holds are all possibly in the list of experiences you would rather forget. Somehow, in all the misery, you still want to be happy. You still want to look forward to tomorrow. You still want that smile on your face like you had at your first dance. You still long to find Joy and purpose, maybe more so than ever before.

You wish you could just escape into the arms of someone who will keep you safe and let you forget about the drama in the world.

I capitalize Joy throughout the book because, to me, J.O.Y. means Jesus, Others, Yourself; an acronym that reminds me to stay focused on those all-important components in the right order. That is how we find Joy. I assure you, with all the crazy things happening today in the world, you can still find Joy. Yes, you need to acknowledge your surroundings, not ignore them. Yes, you need to admit your fear and despair. The key, however, is to recognize the good and embrace it, even when so much seems so bad.

Joy doesn't mean you are happy and dancing around all the time. Trials will come and they will pass. New challenges will be put in your path, but there will always be good things coming in at the same time. Good and bad exists in life and the bad can overpower your mind and emotions so that you are not living a fruitful life. What could possibly keep you consistently happy and filled with Joy?

Many people search their whole lives for this mysterious word we call Joy, as if it is a buried treasure just waiting to be discovered. They bet their lives to search for it. They bury themselves in their work, take on a second or third job to make more money or buy objects of luxury with the money they have. Some attempt to find Joy through escapism with drugs or alcohol. Unfortunately, the treasure remains buried, never to be found.

In reality, true Joy is right in front of you and has been with you all along. Love, Joy, peace, patience, kindness, goodness, gentleness, faithfulness, and self-control are all ingredients to living a fruitful life. Discovering the source of that Joy and growing in it are the foundations of this book.

Joy in itself is only the beginning. A way to live your life exists that brings much Joy, waterfalls of Joy! Yes, there are also waterfalls of trials, but the Joy, the love, always wins out. That level of Joy cannot be bought. It cannot be earned. It can only be given away through something called grace.

Grace is a gift given only by God for you to receive. Think of it like an invitation to dance with Him. All you must do is ask for Him to come into your life and the relationship begins. Whether you were born and raised in the church or have lived life to this point never hearing about God and His gifts, the treasure of Joy is made available to all who ask for it. This book provides a pathway for you to start, or re-ignite, your relationship with God so that you dance with Him, again, or for the first time.

Joyce Meyer (a Christian writer) had a horrible childhood. She suffered sexual abuse from her father until she was a teenager. She found Christ through her seeking and suffering. She was a total naysayer, and God did His work and put His hand in her life.

A very prominent Christian man had a daughter who was raised in the church. To him, she was the perfect Christian daughter. At age 16, she made choices that separated her from God and her family for two years. The power of prayer brought her back to her relationship with God.

A particular young man was a rebel…with a cause! He grew up in the shadow of two prominent evangelist parents, and yet he rebelled constantly as a young adult. He was kicked out of high school for smoking, drinking, and defying authority. He was even expelled from college before finding his way back. Franklin Graham, son of Billy and

Ruth Graham, described his restless youth in his first book *Rebel With a Cause*. Why did Franklin go through all that? To be the kind of person that God had planned for him. Billy, his dad, was an evangelist for a "normal" world. Franklin has been ministering and evangelizing in the third world through his non-profit organization, Samaritan's Purse, because God's plan included Franklin going *against* the norm. He went through his rebellious youth to become the kind of service leader that God planned for him.

Those are just a few of the many examples showing how Christ comes to those who seek Him. If you are feeling broken, down and out, or truly at the end of your rope, this book could be just the vehicle to bring you to Joy. If you are grieving the loss of someone or something that was beloved in your life, you are hurting. You may even be mad at God or have been driven to believe He doesn't exist. This book can provide the restoration of hope you have been looking for.

People have choices and they will either choose God or not. God gave us free will. He works on our hearts. He will hear our hearts. Ultimately God's love is where the power is.

We must follow Him and live a life that says something about Him and contributes to others. The alternative is to become a taker and self-serving. There is no in-between. You have a choice which way you want to go. The Bible talks about that too. There are two roads to take. The path toward righteousness and the path towards self-will. He wants your heart. If He forced you to come to Him, it wouldn't have any value if your heart is broken.

If the time is right in your life to begin, or re-introduce, a relationship with Jesus, I invite you to use my roadmap to help you.

This book contains five main sections that could be used as steps to follow through the journey of discovery in the life of the Lord. You can also refer to specific sections and chapters as a reference point to serve as inspiration. They are:

D–Dare to Dream: *where you resolve to dream the dreams that Jesus already has for you!*

A–Adopt the Almighty: *where you find ways to tap into the power of Jesus.*

N–Nurture Nearness: *where you will learn how to build a relationship with Christ.*

C–Connect to Christ: *where you will discover how to grow your relationship with Christ into a mature, shared connection.*

E–Empower Everyone: *where you share the love of Christ with those around you.*

This message is for you if you want to live a better life, a happier life, a fulfilled life–a life of vitality and purpose, great purpose. God wants you to have a better perspective on your life; a life that gives you energy and a reason to get up in the morning. If we don't have something to wake up for, to look forward to, then why are we on this earth in the first place?

My life is a testimony for Jesus Christ because He is the true Joy giver and He gave me that gift. When I was receiving radiation therapy for breast cancer, He *told* me I was His Joy Giver. As I look back over my entire life, I see how Jesus has been there for me and He is a true Joy. It's been a journey, an exciting...difficult...rewarding...and fun...journey!

I enjoy having fun, don't you? Christ came to bring righteousness, peace, and Joy. He sacrificed His life for that, so that you and I could live a life *full of* righteousness, peace, and Joy, and thereby be an attraction for others to be curious. I look forward to others seeing you and saying, "Gosh, what makes her so happy and energetic? I want to know more about that!"

God has shown me that I must go through some real painful times, some real down times too—and that's part of the journey. If I do not go through those experiences, I'm not allowing myself to acknowledge the pain and the trials. Then, I really am not going to know what true Joy is and who the true Joy Giver is. I've had opportunity to get to know the Lord even deeper and to be in His word. The Bible is such a treasure. Oh my gosh, it's full of promises—thousands! There are thousands of promises in the Word of God that can lift us up and give us hope and encouragement for the day. Several of those promises are highlighted in this book.

I can't promise anybody that if they choose to seek God, their life will turn around. I don't want to be a Positive Pollyanna like I'm making all these promises, and life is always so wonderful. It's not. It's good and bad. It is not about me. The book includes several examples and periods of my life, and my own journey to Christ, but it is really about **finding the true Joy Giver: Jesus.** So, I don't make any promises. People must make decisions for themselves. They need to seek out the treasure that God offers them, and they must make their own decisions. I am not going to force anyone because He does not force anybody. I just want to lead readers of this book to the road where there's light and hope. His scripture is a light to our path.

I honestly do not believe that I would be alive today if my relationship with Him did not begin when it had. I do not believe that I would be able to witness and bring others to Jesus if I had not decided to ask Him for help when I was desperate. My heart was crying out for His help. I knew I was at a turning point where I was either going to choose Him to help me change my life or not.

God's Word promises, *"All things work together for good to those who love God" (Romans 8:28, NKJV)*. What a beautiful promise that is, but sometimes we have to wait. Sometimes it does not look like anything is going to change. I've been there, but I kept seeking Him, praying, and crying out to Him.

Are you ready to meet Him?

Please accept my invitation to find things to laugh about again, and actual steps you can use to find Joy. God has blessed us with a lot of great comedians and funny movies and things to make us lighten up. When our heart is light, we can learn more. That is why it's so imperative to seek and find Joy. Living with Joy in our hearts is not about laughing all the time and being giddy and silly and happy. But laughter is huge. Laughter is so important to physiologically clear our minds and our hearts so that we can receive God's truth. When you are always intense, you're like a pressure cooker. There's no relief, and pretty soon you explode because the pressure just keeps building. Laughter gives a body and mind a release and relief. That's why Christ came again! To bring righteousness, peace, and Joy. When we lighten up, we can hear things. We can see things. We can respond to teaching and be taught.

Are you looking for promises you can rely on? Do you want something to change? Have you ever thought about what it would be like to dig for buried treasure? Finding Joy is an adventure and adventures can be a lot of fun. You don't know exactly what you will find, but curiosity is going to keep you digging and digging. To find what you are looking for, you will discover a little piece here, a little gem there and it will keep you actively searching. Jesus is waiting for you to ask Him to dance with you. Are you willing to take a small leap if it means the discovery of this great treasure?

D.A.N.C.E. WITH HIM

SECTION 1–**D**are to Dream

> *But those who hope in the Lord will renew their strength. They will soar on wings like eagles; they will run and not grow weary, they will walk and not faint. Isaiah 40:31 NIV*

DAR GEIGER

CHAPTER 1
HUNT FOR TREASURE

Laughter surrounded me as I grew up. My parents were young at heart, always dancing and singing. They taught me, my sisters, Annie, Bonnie, and little brother, Bud, that laughter is good medicine.

And did we laugh! Forget television; my family would entertain themselves! I remember one night where we spent three hours doing Elvis Presley imitations. Uh, huh: gyrating hips and all. It was hilarious! Our family was always laughing.

Today, we fall right back into that joyful, playful state when we are together, and I have tried to share that delight with others. It is such a treasure. People crave those feelings of exultation, contentment, and blessedness like a baby craves its bottle.

From Lost to Found

It was a beautiful Sunday morning in October 1960. My fiancé Chuck and I were young and in love. My parents had asked us to take my four-year-old brother to church with us because they had something they needed to do that morning. "No problem!" we assured them, happy to have a reason to be together. Even baby-sitting my little brother was blissful because we wanted to be together all the time.

Do you remember how it feels to be caught up in the early stages of love? Your significant other consumes you–all your energy, focus and time is dedicated to them. It is euphoric! I remember feeling that way on that beautiful October morning driving home after services, cuddled up next to Chuck in the front seat (ah, the days of shelf seats and no seatbelt requirements…). We adored each other. Yes, we were amorous, that was part of the bliss of being in love. Nothing could go wrong.

Until, as we approached our house, my dad came roaring down the street toward us and pulled us over to the side of the road. He rolled down his window and barked, "WHERE'S YOUR BROTHER?"

Good gracious, I forgot my baby brother!

Thank goodness, Bud was fine. The reverend who was going to marry us found him sitting by his Sunday School room crying, "What happened to Dar and Chuck?" Knowing how *fond* we were of each other, he immediately guessed what must have happened and called my dad. Bud jokes about it to this day, how Chuck and I traumatized him for life by forgetting him at the church.

As easy as it was for two young lovers to forget a small child in their infatuation for each other, letting distractions of the world consume you to the point where you forget Joy—and where (who) that joy comes from—is equally easy.

Joy is here. You did not intentionally leave it behind. You just let other things preoccupy you to the point that you forgot how important it is in your life. But Joy is waiting for you. Go find it.

Finding Joy

Whether you are looking for Joy for the first time, or remember it and desperately want it back, I am here to tell you it is waiting for you. You can find Joy.

"But wait, Dar, I have no idea what to look for! It has been so long (or never) since I felt any Joy, I don't even know where to begin."

Let's take a treasure hunt, shall we? Joy is a treasure absolutely worth searching for.

Imagine you are visiting a flea market, and you come across an old box. It is dusty and grimy and has been sitting there, unopened for years, waiting for someone to discover it.

That someone is you. Do you dare open it? You reach out tentatively, nervous over what might be inside. Slowly, you open the lid.

What do you see?

Money?

Old clothes?

Photographs?

When I went on a similar treasure hunt, I found a book. The pages were full of stories of trials and triumph, failure and victory, brokenness and forgiveness.

It contained the stories of some of the wealthiest people in the world, and some of the poorest.

It had stories of mystery, intrigue, love, betrayal, hate, loyalty, and more.

It included letters from people in prison and others safe and secure at home, surrounded by people they loved.

Although the book's stories and letters were diverse in the characters and their circumstances, there was one underlying message: Joy!

The Joy-filled treasure I discovered was the Bible.

As a God-appointed agent of Joy, I can assure you that you will not find it in a new car, a big house, or lots of money in the bank. None of those things prevent you from finding Joy, but this book I found is not about worldly success. It is about Joy; what Jesus came to give us. Righteousness, peace, and Joy! The book was provided to us so that we can thrive and live life like it is a hunt for buried treasure. And the prize is in the Bible.

> *For the Kingdom of God is not a matter of eating and drinking, but of righteousness, peace, and joy in the Holy Spirit. Romans 14:17 NIV*

Nevertheless, the world does its best to make you believe otherwise. It becomes your enemy, doing everything it can to make you feel unimportant and worth nothing, cheap, discounted. The enemy wants to suck the Joy out of you and leave you feeling empty and alone. He wants to replace feelings of cheerfulness and glee with agony and depression; to yank your purpose right out of you and coerce you into believing your life has no meaning.

That is what the enemy does. There were many times in my life when I succumbed to the enemy's wicked bantering. I turned to earthly solutions to replace the Joy I remembered from my childhood, including alcohol abuse and misconduct. My discovery was that none of those temporary fixes bring Joy.

Once I overcame the worldly assailant and embraced Joy again, the battles with the enemy continued. The attack shifted to the ones I love.

Janet's Story

> *Come to me, all you who are weary and burdened, and I will give you rest. Matthew 11: 28 NIV*

I have known Janet for many years. I missed her the other day, so I picked up the phone to call. As soon as she heard my voice, she said, "I'm so glad you called, Dar, because I have to ask you for forgiveness." That took me by surprise because I was unaware of anything there to forgive.

Janet explained that she felt terrible about not reaching out a few months earlier when Vito, my partner of several years, died. Janet said she had escaped entirely from my life after Vito's death, even though I was grieving. She knew I had support from my family, and she didn't want to burden me with her problems. Janet went through a dark patch in her life with her children and husband, an alcoholic. She shut down emotionally to cope with the pain, rather than reaching out for support.

"I could not contact you," Janet explained." I couldn't reach out to anyone. I just went into limbo and went dark for a long time. I felt helpless and desperate and could barely function."

I know those feelings. Emotionally, spiritually, physically, you just shut down. You cannot handle even one more thing. However, let me share that the enemy wants you to shut down emotionally in times of grief and depression.

Those are the perfect times for personal character assassination attempts that can wipe out your self-esteem and suck the Joy right out of you.

The truth is, life is filled with unbearable pain, and it can seem simpler to shut down emotionally than deal with it. The hope we can cling to is the promise of eternal life. I have no clue how wonderful it will be, but the Bible promises that *"there will be no more death or mourning or crying or pain" (Revelation 21:4 NIV)*. Cling to that promise to help you get through the tough times. God wants us to have *"righteousness, peace, and Joy in the Holy Spirit" (Romans 14:17 NIV)*. Knowing there is somebody on your side more significant than yourself will help you get through whatever you are going through. Janet and I spoke some more, and I made sure she knew that I understood her pain and loved her. I urged her to continue to reach out, even in her sadness, to God and to me as her friend. She would find her Joy again.

Mary Magdalene

I recently saw a fantastic series on the life of Jesus called *"The Chosen."* It was written from the perspective of the people who crossed paths with Jesus. The way the series portrayed Mary Magdalene was so powerful for me; it hit close to home in so many ways.

In the series, various ordeals in Mary Magdalene's life tortured her mentally and physically. She had been raped and abused and tormented by demons. In one powerful scene, Mary found herself on the edge of a cliff, ready to take her life because she could not endure another moment.

Just as she was about to jump, the Holy Spirit appeared in the form of a dove. It drew her attention away from the edge of the cliff and saved her life. The next scene shows Mary in a tavern about to start drinking when she meets Jesus, who tells her to stop. Mary was frightened and choked out, "who are you?" before racing out the door of the tavern. Jesus followed and called her name. "Mary, you don't have to be afraid." She stopped and turned toward Jesus. He went to her and held her face saying, "you belong to me."

The scene is impactful and meaningful to many people who are plagued mentally and emotionally, for those who are calling out for someone to love them–despite everything. Jesus is that someone who longs for you to discover Him.

Joy is Jesus

> *For where your treasure is, there your heart will be also. Matthew 6: 21 NIV*

Do you feel like Janet? Or Mary Magdalene?

Are you emotionally drained? Shut down? Unsure what your purpose is?

Does it feel like everything has changed–what you wanted and worked toward six months or a year ago is futile and unimportant?

Have you lost (or never found) Joy?

My friend, know this, without a shadow of a doubt:

No matter where you have been or where you are in your life now, you can find Joy and make a difference.

You do not have to be happy to have Joy in your life, but you do need to dare to dream.

Joy is an issue of the heart. That is the treasure you seek.

Joy is hope.

Joy is faith.

Joy is a promise.

Joy is a connection.

Joy is love.

Joy is Jesus.

Joy comes from loving people and empowering them to grasp the Joy already in their hearts to make a difference. That is what Christ did. He loved people and empowered them through grace and forgiveness. What a treasure to find out that you are forgiven and loved. Jesus wants you to thrive. You do not have to be wealthy or happy to have Joy. You need to dare to dream the dreams that Jesus already has for you. You must be willing to walk in faith and trust in the Kingdom for your Joy, rather than the world; to do something different than you have always done in the past.

Are you willing to do something different? Then let's go hunt for some treasure together!

DAR GEIGER

CHAPTER 2
JUMP TO JOY

I am the vine; you are the branches. If you remain in me and I in you, you will bear much fruit; apart from me, you can do nothing.
John 15:5 NIV

When I was a little girl, I was so curious. Everything I saw or heard made me ask another question. I wanted to understand everything. I was like a sponge. When I was nine years old, I went to Sunday school class, asking the teacher questions about everything. She would tell me, "We don't ask questions here." That impacted me for years. I learned that it was not okay to be curious.

You may be thinking, what a terrible thing for a teacher to say! It was, but I suspect there are plenty of others who have had their thirst to know squelched by a person of authority. If you have children of your own, you have probably heard these questions:

What's that smell?

Did you swallow the baby?

How deep is that puddle?

Why are there swear words if I am forbidden to say them?

Young children grow through their early years with such curiosity about the world. They want to know about everything! Have you ever thought about why kids lose interest in the unknown as they age? The answer might be for the same reason as to why so many adults lose interest in seeking a relationship with God.

Consider this for a moment. You were created to be curious at birth. However, as you have aged, your simple curiosity was replaced by the people who surrounded you during your growth years. You learned what they wanted you to learn.

Over time, you were raised to become nervous and skeptical about connecting with people and asking them about their lives, feelings, and emotions. Maybe you have even been personally accused of invading someone's privacy. You may remember someone saying to you, "That's none of your business."

No wonder why children seem so full of Joy while adults are always searching endlessly for happiness. Young children may have not yet encountered roadblocks to awareness, such as self-doubt, hesitancy, and anxiety. Kids are often sheltered by their parents from colliding with the enemy. As the stress of teenage years creeps in, your Joy fades.

There is an energy behind curiosity. There is a drive. Curiosity involves wanting to know more because it makes you feel accomplished, and even happy, when you make a discovery on your own. You believe the information is going to help you. By the way, I am not talking only about formal education. I, myself, am self-educated. I worked hard to get what I call my P.H.T. (putting hubby through), but I never went to college. You may feel that if you do not have a formal education that you are not smart enough, that you don't know enough, but those thoughts are lies and limiting beliefs. Guess who planted those thoughts? The enemy.

I know this because I have felt the negative anxiety and lived with self-doubt. Those limiting beliefs that I was somehow not worthy of Joy gave me plenty of pain and tragedy in my life. Today, I realize that all those painful experiences contributed to the opening of my heart to Jesus. I became more curious and wanted to know why I had so much Joy at one point in my life, and so little Joy later.

I was led to study and memorize scripture. I prayed and asked to be directed to a resource to help me. I visited a Christian bookstore and found a taped program in the children's section called "Hiding God's Word in Your Heart," on memorizing scripture. I bought that tape, listened to it, daily, for a year, and learned and personalized 13 scripture passages. From there, it became easier to receive God's word because I discovered that the Bible is an endless treasure and contains everything we need to overcome trials. It is right for today, whatever day that is, and whatever challenges today happens to bring.

Here is what I want to tell you if you are struggling to find your Joy right now. Whether you were joyful in the past and lost it or have never felt Joy, I assure you that you are not alone. You do not have to do this on your own. Jesus is the vine, and you are the branch that will grow and flourish under His care. When His word is in you, you will bear fruit. But without Him? Self-will can bring havoc. You will never find real gratification until you begin to pursue a relationship in God.

I see my relationship with Jesus as Him being the hand and I am the glove. By myself, as a glove, I can't do anything, but Jesus, being the hand, can do everything. Without the hand, I can do nothing, but if I put Jesus on, I am empowered to do all that Jesus would have me do.

You might be asking, "How do I get more curious, Dar?"

> *If you believe, you will receive whatever you ask for in prayer. Matthew 21:22 NIV*

Asking that question has just started you on the road to becoming more curious, and, ultimately, more Joyful in life. One question leads to another, then another, and another.

So, just like a young child, whose curiosity has not yet been repressed, ask questions.

And then ask some more.

If the idea of asking other people questions is scary to you, begin by asking yourself a few. You might want a pen and paper handy to record your answers as well:

> Am I craving something new? What? Why is that important to me?

> Am I willing to do something different?

> Am I feeling adventurous?

> What can I do that would empower me and give me energy?

> Can I take a risk on the unknown? Is it important enough? Am I important enough?

> Do I dare to dream again?

My daughter, Heather, has been through a personal hell, and, by God's grace, has emerged a new woman. It took a lot of courage and commitment for Heather to dream again.

When you go through a debilitating life trial, you long for someone to wave a magic wand and make it go away. The desire for immediate resolution increases when someone you love is hurting. I was so desperate to help my daughter, and I didn't know what to do. My heart was breaking.

A wise friend of mine, Bob, reminded me that Heather was not alone. She was going through what could be the biggest challenge of her life. Still, she had the potential to become the extraordinary person God wanted her to be when she came through it. "Hang on to that," Bob advised. "You might not be able to make it better for Heather, but Someone can."

The impact of those words! I hung on to the promise that God can do all things, and I became a spiritual warrior for my daughter. God knew that I wanted my children to thrive, and, while I could not fix it myself, He could. I started spiritual warfare on behalf of Heather, trusting that no matter how I feel, what I see, or what I don't see, God said it, He will do it, and that's it! No ifs, ands, or buts. My prayers were the glove—God reached out His hand, filled up that glove, and answered my prayers.

How it comes out is what matters, in the end, although you cannot skip to the back of the book to learn the happy ending when you are still in the desert. All you can do to get through it is ask the questions, have faith, and trust that someone greater than yourself loves you unconditionally and wants you to find your Joy.

Dare to believe it.

You are not broken. No, you are not.

God loves you.

God said it. He will do it. That is it.

Dare to believe it.

Dare to dream.

Go get your Joy!

Take Action!

> *Dear children, let us not love with words or speech but with actions and in truth.*
> *1 John 3:18 NIV*

Everybody wants a quick fix, but a transformation to life filled with Joy does not happen overnight. It took a long time to get you to where you are today, desperate and on the hunt for Joy. If you want a different life, you must be willing to do something different. Crave doing something different.

I want you to know that you have significance.

You have an incredible story.

You have something incredible to contribute.

You will find Joy in action; in investment—investment in yourself and other people.

I know from my growing up with a family of alcoholics how people can change. I understand how people can thrive despite their circumstances. I have been sober for 33 years, thank the Lord. My husband recovered and had 20 joyful years free of the chains of alcoholism before he died. There is Joy in that—in seeing yourself and others change.

If you want to find Joy, you have to dig for the treasure. Jesus said, *"Keep on asking, and you will receive what you ask for. Keep on seeking, and you will find. Keep on knocking, and the door will be opened to you. For everyone who asks, receives. Everyone who seeks, finds. And to everyone who knocks, the door will be opened." (Matthew 7: 7-8 NLT).* Rise to the challenge to find Joy in your life. Go find it.

Investments take time. Investments take commitment. Investments take guts.

You must invest in yourself. Start now by taking action and investing in yourself.

Jesus Christ invested in us. He gave His life for us. He lived thirty-some years on this earth, investing in teaching other people of His love, grace, and mercy. Then He suffered unimaginable pain and torture on the cross, giving His entire life for us, so that we can thrive and live fruitful lives.

He wants us to live lives that matter and make a difference.

If someone loves you so much, to invest everything for you, don't you think you have value? That you are here for more than mediocre? That you are significant?

But are you doing it? Are you taking action? Make that investment. Go find your Joy.

You cannot find it alone. Thank the Lord that you don't have to try alone! Jesus is the hand in the glove. He does the work; all you must do is lift the glove and allow Him to fill it, to empower you. Rely upon and trust in Him to bring you to fruition.

> **For where two or three gather in my name, there am I with them. Matthew 18:20 NIV**

Jesus invested in us with His life, and that atonement gives us a deep-down desire to invest in others.

Thinking about and bringing value to others is very rewarding. Our lives are empty without it.

God made us for relationships—relationships with other people and a relationship with God. He wants us to come to Him, tell Him what we need, and lean on Him for support. And He wants us to do the same for others. That's why we are here. No man is an island. Relationships matter. They can hurt, too. It hurts when you lose a loved one or discover that someone betrayed you or tried to break you. It can suck the Joy right out of you. But to dare to dream, we need to be willing to take that risk. Despite those who wound up hurting me, I'm so grateful for all the relationships God blessed me with in life.

About two years ago, I attended an event led by Susan Runnels for her organization called "Your Second Season." Susan formed the support group to encourage those going through menopause, a tough time in any woman's life.

The Holy Spirit orchestrates many of my meetings with women, and I know that God wants me to reach out to them so He can bless us. My meeting Susan was one of those instances. I felt drawn to her, so I asked her to meet me for coffee after the event. It took no more than an hour to realize we were kindred spirits and would be friends for life. That type of connection does not happen very often. It's a rare thing but when it does, it is electric. We continued our friendship, and it turned out that Susan had been thirsting to learn about the Holy Spirit. I was so delighted! She later shared that she had been praying for someone to come into her life to trust, someone who wanted to teach, encourage, and empower her. Someone who could help her find her Joy again. I was happy to help, but I knew who brought us together when it comes right down to it. I am the glove. God filled it and reached out to Susan. We are very dear friends now and know all about each other, the good and the bad. That's the Joy of living a life for Christ. He knows who and what we need in our lives before we do. All we have to do is sit back, accept where God leads us, and enjoy the journey.

Relationships are key. I'm not saying that relationships are important. I'm saying that they are invaluable! They are a treasure that brings so much Joy into your life. Throughout history, there are stories of real people who triumphed over tragedy, wrote beautiful music or inspiring literature. These people were able to contribute such beautiful works because they had at least one person in their life that made them feel as if they had purpose and meaning. Someone that made them realize they could make a difference. Relationships encourage, affirm, and inspire.

Forming relationships with other people helps you get over yourself and your problems and serve others. Over the years, I have learned that it does not pay to sit on the pity-pot for long because you just get a ring around your bum. Serving others is so much more rewarding and brings so much Joy. Sure, you will have ups and downs. Not every relationship you invest in will thrive. But relationships are

God's way of reaching out to those who have not met Him yet. When His love comes through and helps just one person, it brings such Joy.

DAR GEIGER

CHAPTER 3
BE OPEN TO THE IMPOSSIBLE

> *Jesus looked at them and said, "With man, this is impossible, but with God all things are possible."*
> *Matthew 19:26 NIV*

Rebecca's Story

Rebecca was born in China, moved to Canada, married, and had a son. She never knew God, and when I met her, she was desperate and alone. Rebecca's abusive husband took their son, left her in Canada, and moved to Omaha, Nebraska. Rebecca was isolated and desperately lonely. She felt powerless to fight her abusive husband. She did what she could to scrape up enough money to visit her son in Omaha as often as possible.

One day, God stepped in with a "coincidence." I say that in jest because there is never a coincidence in God's Kingdom. He orchestrates everything.

That day, Rebecca was in Omaha and took her son to the zoo. My girlfriend and I were there with her child and my grandson. In the gorilla house, my grandson ran over to greet Rebecca's boy. They knew each other! They went to the same preschool.

It was clear that Rebecca was alone and longed to belong. The compassion bubbled up, and my friend and I invited her and her little guy to have lunch with us. She accepted. One thing led to another, and we ended up spending most of her week-long stay with Rebecca. We connected relationally, attended Bible study with each other, and supported her through a very nasty episode with her ex.

I cannot help but see God's hand in our glove when we met Rebecca. What are the chances that my grandson went to the same preschool as her son? There are a lot of preschools in Omaha! What made us decide to go to the zoo on the same day they did or to see the gorillas at the same time? What if we hadn't invited Rebecca to lunch? Rebecca was a desperately lonely woman with no hope, powerless to fight on her own against an abusive ex. God gave her hope, encouragement, and love through us, resulting in so much Joy! What we think is impossible, God makes possible.

Whose role do you relate to in the story?

Are you Rebecca, longing and praying for someone to see you and hear you, someone to be your friend? If you feel like you are alone and abandoned, be ready for the impossible. Be open and prepared for someone whom God places in your life that you will soon meet. When they ask you for lunch or coffee, be willing to say yes. Dare to dream again.

Or do you relate to my friend and me, faced with the opportunity to make a difference in someone's life? Don't slam the door on God's opportunity because you had other plans. Reach out that glove and pass on God's love through your friendship.

Maybe you relate to my grandson—just surprised to see a friend in an unusual place. Don't duck your head and hide. Run over and greet them! You never know where it might lead.

Okay, you say you relate to the gorilla, just looking for a banana. By all means, stop at the grocery store on your way home and get a banana. While you're at it, get a bunch and share with your new friends.

Joy comes from relationships. Relationships come from possibilities. Grasping those possibilities leads to Joy. Do you see how, no matter where you are today, even if you feel alone and isolated, you can find Joy again?

God meets you where you are

He said to me, "My grace is sufficient for you, for my power is made perfect in weakness."
2 Corinthians 12:9 NIV

But Dar, you may say, you are something else. You are so bubbly and know where you are going in life. You are happy and driven. It makes sense that God would seek you out. I'm just a regular person. I've done some terrible things. There is no room in God's day to orchestrate a miracle just to bring me happiness. I am not even sure I deserve to be happy or have Joy in my life.

I want you to know that God doesn't think that way. He meets you where you are, as long as you are ready to connect with Him. I didn't form a real relationship with Him until I had done some pretty terrible things. I always knew there was a God because I was baptized and raised as a Christian. However, I didn't have a personal relationship with Him. I was running on the steam of my self-will, and it was unfulfilling, and frankly, disastrous. I felt as though I was going crazy at times, always seeking self-satisfaction, and making choices that were hurtful to myself and others. My choices did not gratify. They did not satisfy. I was bouncing off the walls emotionally. I knew what I should do, but didn't want to do it. I wanted to do what I wanted to do, even though I knew it was wrong. My emotions were running my life. When I think back to my life BC (before Christ), I honestly thought my life would soon end. The things I was doing were so dangerous and life-threatening.

I prayed:

"God. I'm desperate. I'm scared to death that I'm going to die. I know I need You. I need something. I need help. My life is a mess. Please. Please provide something to help me change my life and change my ways. I don't want to live like this anymore. Amen."

You know, God did not care where I was. He didn't wait until I was the Dar I am today. He met me where I was (and it was not a good place, believe me). Instead of ignoring me, He helped me find my Joy to become the Dar I am today. What Joy!

What is the opposite of Joy? Pain, hurt, embarrassment, shame, loneliness. These are feelings that push us. They force us to the point where we choose one of two options. We either give up entirely or seek the opposite of those feelings (Joy) with all our hearts. When you reach that place, where you are open and willing to seek Him out, He meets you there. *Ask and it will be given to you; seek and you will find; knock and the door will be opened to you. (Matthew 7:7 NLT)*.

God Leaves No One Behind

> *Truly my soul finds rest in God; my salvation comes from him. Truly he is my rock and my salvation; he is my fortress; I will never be shaken. Psalm 62: 1-2 NLT*

David was the apple of God's eye. God anointed him a king before others saw more than a boy, a harp, and some sheep. God saw his potential. Still, David messed up. He sinned terribly. David fell for Bathsheba, another guy's wife. He killed her husband so he could have her to himself. They had a child who died. Another son, Absalom, hated David so much he tried to kill him for years. David was in pain. Pain from knowing he had messed up, pain from missing his child, pain because he lost his Joy when he lost track of God. David poured out his pain in the psalms. He cried out to God to meet him where he was, heal, and bring back the Joy. "Don't forget about me, God," he would beg, "help me finish well!" That prayer kept him spiritually well. Despite all his emotional trials, David tenaciously hung on to something greater than himself. And in the end, he found his Joy. He finished well.

Do you dare to dream?

I want to share with you a bit of HiStory. That is, His story where God made a lasting impression on my life, so that I could share it with others. You may not believe it. I certainly don't understand it. But it is HiStory. And so, I trust it to be true.

HiStory begins in 2006, when my husband, Chuck, suffered a massive heart attack, and after an eight-week battle, the Lord took him home. I knew Chuck was with Christ in Heaven, yet I functioned in a dark cloud for several years. I was afraid of death. I became obsessed with how death would find me. My fear became an idol that dominated my thoughts and overshadowed my Joy.

In July, 2010, I listened to a Chuck Swindoll lesson on confessing your idolatries. His words convicted me, and I admitted to God that I was terrified over how I would die. I told him that my fear was ruling me and keeping me from knowing the Lord and his love. I asked God to forgive me. I cried out that I didn't want idols to rule my life and begged Him for help.

In August of that year, I was diagnosed with breast cancer. All of a sudden, my calendar was full of chemotherapy treatments and surgery. Talk about a prayer answered differently than I expected! I was hoping God would give me peace, and I got cancer instead. Nevertheless, I chose to see cancer as the little c and Christ as the big C!

I prayed on my own, with family, and my Bible study women. At one friend's suggestion, I meditated on the resurrecting healing blood of Christ moving through my veins and dissolving harmful, cancerous blood with healing protection.

I had 15 lymph nodes removed, and eight were cancerous. The next step was a lumpectomy. It went very well, and I felt pretty good when Heather came to take me home from the hospital. We were sitting in the car when she looked over at me and said, "Mom, you're bleeding!"

I was hemorrhaging, and I didn't even know it. Heather turned the car around and took me back to the hospital's emergency room. As she helped me inside, I felt lightheaded.

As I tried to sit down, I said, "Jesus, help me," and passed out. The last thing I heard was Heather screaming for a doctor.

While I was passed out, I saw three silhouettes of light around me and had an incredible feeling of peace, love, and Joy. It was indescribable love and Joy. I remember saying, "can I please stay?"

Then I regained consciousness, and people were helping me onto a stretcher. I was hemorrhaging profusely, and they admitted me to intensive care. I told Heather and Chuck Jr. that God visited me with a glimpse of what it is going to be like in Heaven and that it is fantastic. Indescribable. It's true what His word says: *"No eye has seen, no ear has heard, and no mind has imagined what God has prepared for those who love Him." (1 Corinthians 2:9 NLT).* That experience stripped my fear of death away.

I prayed to God to remove the fear of death that was ruling me and show me how to focus on Him. I think God knows me and provided me with what I needed. That is HiStory.

If you are hurting or fearful or anxious about something, I encourage you to dare to dream. If you want your life to change, I challenge you to take a risk. Ask God to speak to you. I know He will talk to you personally. Your contact point might not be in the same exact way as He revealed himself to me after surgery or how He may communicate with someone else. No. God loves you personally and knows what you need. God wants his children to ask Him for help. It's up to you to make the first move. Cry out to God to meet you.

What is your prayer?

> *In you, Lord, I have taken refuge; let me never be put to shame. In your righteousness, rescue me, and deliver me; turn your ear to me and save me. Psalm 71:1-2 NIV*

Communicating with God is nothing more than a prayer. David prayed constantly. Perhaps you aren't sure what to pray yet. You dare to dream, but still have no idea where to begin. You feel broken, alone, and mentally and spiritually empty. How can you dance to Joy when it feels like your kneecaps are broken?

How do you go from feeling empty, desperate, and at a loss, to open, receiving, and grateful? How do you choose Joy over pain? The answer begins with one tiny action step that will not cost you a penny. And it requires only a few moments of your time.

Are you willing to take real action right now to begin to find Joy in your life?

If you are in a place with no one else around, please pray the following prayer with me out loud. If you are in a busy place with people everywhere, ignore your surroundings for a moment and pray this prayer to yourself silently:

"Dear God, I'm at a loss. I feel alone and desperate. Scared. I'm reaching out to you. Please help me. Show me that You are there. Give me a sign, so I have something to hang onto. Give me hope for something more than what's going on in my life right now. I need You. I need encouragement. Help me. Amen."

Yes, prayer can be as simple as "God, if You're there, please help. Please show up. Amen."

You can live a life of vitality through all the trials, sorrows, and painful times. There is light in the dark, and despite the pain in the world, there are wonderfully good things to find Joy in today. Ask God to show you what is good with today. The sky is clear and beautiful. The sun is out, the trees are green. A baby is born. An older person dies with their loving family nearby, freed at last from sickness and pain and home with their Father in Heaven. The Bible is full of promises, and they are worth hanging onto.

God will meet you where you are and will also provide you with what you need. When I called out to God in my desperate prayer, He was right there, even though I did not see Him or hear Him or feel Him, because I'm His child. I didn't think anybody was there who could help me. I felt so alone when all the time, there was Jesus. I just had to let my heart break and to say, "help me."

Suddenly, resources began piling up, which helped me focus on Jesus and find my Joy again. I would hear just the right song on the radio or read a scripture suitable to lead me to my next step in the journey. In the next section, I will share how you can find resources to search for Joy.

I hope you see now that you are here for a reason, and that reason is to find your Joy and share it with others in rich and beautiful ways. God will answer your heart's cry for help. Wait. Look for it. Listen. You will find it.

FOR REFLECTION: SECTION 1
Dare to Dream

- ♥ What do you treasure in life?
- ♥ How can you tell if something is missing inside you?
- ♥ Do you feel a hole in your heart and can't find anything to fill it?
- ♥ How have you tried to fill the emptiness so far?
- ♥ What are your options?
- ♥ When are you going to take action?
- ♥ Did you know that action cures fear?
- ♥ Are you willing to brave it and take a risk?
- ♥ What do you think it will take to experience vitality and a life well lived?
- ♥ Do you recall an experience in your life when God might have been present, and you didn't realize it until now?

DAR GEIGER

D.**A**.N.C.E. WITH HIM

SECTION 2–**A**dopt the Almighty

And I am certain that God, who began the good work within you, will continue His work until it is finally finished on the day when Christ Jesus returns. Philippians 1:6 NLT

DAR GEIGER

CHAPTER 4
WHAT DO YOU NEED
TO THRIVE?

I did not have an easy childhood. I was sick often and missed school. We were fairly poor and lived in houses provided by our church. While we were grateful for the shelter, sometimes the homes lacked hot water for baths and had rodents. The advantage was that we would help my dad clean the church that was providing our house, and then we were allowed to play the organ or piano. That was important to us because despite our troubles, there was always one thing that ministered to our family. That motivation was music, dancing, and singing.

My mom and dad danced together all the time. She told me that she refused even to date my dad until he learned how to dance. Well, he did learn, and they became great dancers together. I remembered that maneuver and gave Chuck the same conditions when he was courting me. We spent a large portion of my time growing up in our home dancing and playing music. Music uplifted and energized us. It made us happy. My mom and dad loved the big band music from the 1940s. We kids had some crazy funny songs in the 50s and 60s, such as The Flying Purple People Eater, Itsy Bitsy Teenie Weenie Yellow Polka Dot Bikini, or Yellow Submarine. We would hear those songs and just laugh!

My children grew up with music and dancing. I would bounce my babies on my lap along with the music before they could even walk. We used to watch Lawrence Welk together as a family, and Chuck and I would dance along. The kids would jump up and join us.

I still have to dance. Some people go jogging or do yoga first thing in the morning. I dance! My mind and body crave dancing. I turn on my favorite music, take 20 minutes, and dance around my home. The house is a ranch style, so I have lots of room to move. After I have done my morning dance to Joy, I feel so much better! Music is good for the soul, mind, will, and emotions.

I have discovered that I need music and dancing in my life to thrive. Maybe many of you reading this book feel the same. When we listen to pleasurable music, the "pleasure chemical" dopamine is released in the striatum, a crucial part of the brain's reward system. The feelings that result are the same feelings you might receive from food, sex, or laughter–activities that are critical to survival.

Music alone is not the answer to Joy, however. If that were the case, I would merely need to provide you with a playlist and send you on your way. Music can provoke other feelings, too, such as anxiety, boredom, and even anger. Music has a history. A song playing during a bad breakup, a car accident, or some other traumatic event will not bring Joy when you hear it the next time–or even 10 or 20 years later. The negative emotions linger.

Admitting that you have a problem (that made you lose your Joy) is the first step of courage

> *You turned my wailing into dancing; you removed my sackcloth and clothed me with joy, that my heart may sing your praises and not be silent. Psalm 30: 11-12 NLT*

I recently mentored a young single mom with an alcohol problem. The daughter of a friend of mine, she was willing to talk to me to make her mom happy. She came over to my home for lunch. As we ate, she shared her story. She knew she was making mistakes. She had trouble resisting alcohol's temptation. She would do well for a while, avoiding the allure, and then out of the blue, she would abandon her resolve and give in.

It may not be alcohol that is stripping you of your Joy. You have a personal weakness that the enemy uses to snare you into thinking you will never be happy without it. Maybe it is shopping, control, food, sex, worry, anxiety, or overwork. Everyone has a lure that keeps them from their Joy. The enemy knows that as long as you are trapped into thinking that you need that lure to be happy, you will never find real Joy–Joy in the Lord.

As our lunch progressed, the young woman I was mentoring admitted to me she had a problem. That's when

I knew we were getting somewhere because if there is one thing I have learned, it is that you have to admit you have a problem. When you are miserable and want something else out of life, what are your other choices? You can drink, you can go out to bars. You can be sexually active to cover up your pain. You can overeat or gamble. People turn to lures to cover up their pain.

Covering up your pain will not release you from it. Strongholds are a mask to keep you from turning to the one thing that will bring real Joy–Jesus Christ. So many people do not find the Joy in Jesus until they are hurting badly. Jesus wants you to make a choice. God gave you the freedom to say and do whatever you want. Our stubborn natures mean that you often have to hit rock-bottom–get so sick and tired of being sick and tired–so desperate–that you cry out, "I can't do this anymore! I need help!"

> *May the God of hope fill you with all Joy and peace as you trust in him, so that you may overflow with hope by the power of the Holy Spirit. Romans 15:13 NIV*

Have Courage

My mentee left our lunch committed to making a change. She agreed to talk to my AA sponsor and was encouraged. I haven't heard from her since. I know she never connected with my sponsor. I have tried to reach out and see how she is doing but have gotten no response. I suspect she is still struggling, but I continue to pray for her. My timing is not God's timing. In AA, we have a saying: It takes what it takes. I can't control any of that. People must make a choice, and that takes courage.

I want you to understand that: Joy takes courage! It takes guts. You don't have to be brave to keep doing what you are already doing, then feeling sorry for yourself and basking in your misery. That isn't brave. That is giving in.

It takes courage to say, "I need to change. I want something different in my life because I am miserable. I see other people with Joy, and I want that!"

Meeting Vito

> *Trust in the Lord with all your heart; do not depend on your own understanding. Seek his will in all you do, and he will show you which path to take. Proverbs 3: 5-6 NLT*

I didn't dance for many years after my husband, Chuck, passed. I lost my Joy when he died. We were celebrating our 45th anniversary when he had a heart attack. He lasted for eight weeks before the Lord said it was time for him to come home. After 53 years together, that was a blow. For three years, I was lost and didn't want to live. My family and friends helped me through that time. Nevertheless, for seven years, my Joy, while still there, felt muffled. I rarely danced.

That was until I met Mr. Vito in 2014. I had been a widow for seven years and was longing for connection—not romantically, and not necessarily with men. I was just praying for the discernment to find people with whom I could develop meaningful relationships. The night I met Vito, I was out to dinner with my two girlfriends, Barb and Connie, celebrating Barb's birthday. Anthony's restaurant had a dance room with live music, and Barb wanted to dance for her birthday.

Vito's wife had passed two years earlier and, although he didn't frequent bars regularly, he felt drawn to stop in at Anthony's that night to see how the dancing was. My friend Connie knew Vito and invited him over to dance. "Oh, Vito's here," she exclaimed. "He is such a great guy and a terrific dancer. He will dance with you for your birthday, Barb!" She called him over, and he danced with Barb, and then he danced with me. It was a good dance–it was fun. He had come to the U.S. from Italy when he was 19 and never lost his accent. I loved that accent.

As we sat down after dancing, Connie turned into a matchmaker and urged me to give Vito my phone number. He chimed in and said in his Italian accent, "Yes, please. I would love a dance partner. Do you want to go dancing sometime?"

I was scared to death sitting there. I didn't want to give out my phone number to a man–I didn't even know him. It had been a long time since Chuck died, and I wasn't looking for a man in my life. Surely this dancing Italian could not have been God's answer to my prayers, could he? It was so not what I had in mind.

Finally, after much cajoling, I gave Vito my business card but was still thinking, no, I'm not interested.

Three days later, not long after I had prayed for discernment into finding more ways to connect with people, Vito called me. This time, I didn't ignore God's nudge. I got to know Vito, and he turned out to be such a blessing in my life. He was so lovely; I don't think he had an enemy in the world. He was hopeless after his wife died. He wanted to die. In one of our early conversations, Vito confided that he had been asking God to take him home. "Then," he said affectionately, "there was Darlena."

As much as I helped Vito to recover from his wife's death, he helped me recharge my Joy during a difficult time. I see now how God orchestrated our meeting to bring dancing back to my life; to bring back Joy. We had four years of just exquisite dancing–ballroom dancing, the tango, the waltz, and the jitterbug. We just "jived" together, both on the dance floor and off.

I was terrified to step away from my "comfort zone" and take a chance with Vito. Even though I had been praying for connection and relationship, when God presented me with an answer to that prayer, I almost ignored it and walked away. Let me repeat; Joy takes courage! It takes guts. You don't have to be brave to keep doing what you are already doing. That isn't brave.

Jesus wants you to make a choice. Will you continue with what is comfortable and familiar to you even though you long for something more? Or will you make a choice to start a relationship with Jesus? Have the courage to initiate one. Believe me when I tell you that you do not have to be perfect to have a relationship. God will meet you where you are. If you take a step toward God, He will climb mountains for you. He loves you that much.

Even if you are unsure about all of this yet, you can pray anyway. If you have not accepted God into your life, you can pray anyway. If you have not yet determined whether I am onto something, or just another religious nut, I encourage you to pray anyway, with the expectation that something good is going to happen.

Have courage. Take the risk. Pray: "God, if you're here, show me. I need to see You."

I mean, what do you have to lose? The same place, stuck where you are already.

What do you have to gain? A happier, Joy-filled life.

Have courage!

CHAPTER 5
COURAGEOUS COLLATERAL

Stand your ground, putting on the belt of truth and the body armor of God's righteousness. For shoes, put on the peace that comes from the Good News so that you will be fully prepared. In addition to all of these, hold up the shield of faith to stop the devil's fiery arrows. Put on salvation as your helmet, and take the sword of the Spirit, which is the Word of God.
Ephesians 6: 14-17 NLT

When a person buys a house, the bank lending the money will use the home as collateral. The bank is a business, and if they lose too much money on loans that do not get paid back, they will soon go out of business. The collateral ensures that the bank can keep operating even if the loans don't get paid back every time.

Being courageous all the time is difficult, especially when life is hard. It's easy to say, "Be brave! Take a risk!" It is even easy to be brave and sometimes take a risk, but you cannot expect to do it long term without a little collateral to help ensure it. Zig Ziglar, a Christian business motivator, was known for saying, *"Everyone says motivation doesn't last. Well, neither does bathing. That's why we do it daily."*

Some resources can help you find your Joy. Some are available to start right now, this minute, and others may take a bit more work. Let's look at a few now.

Prayer

In the last chapter, we said that the first step of courage is often crying out to God for help, even if you are not sure there is a God to listen to you. "God, maybe you are there, I don't know for sure, but I'd like to find out if there is something more. Are You there?" Prayer is always available to you and will never run out of supply.

God has placed an absolute desire and passion in each of our souls (mind, will, and emotions) to have a relationship with Him. In God's mind, a relationship with Him is not just an important thing to do, or even high on the priority list, but is as vital as the need for water to survive! He gave us the powerful gift of prayer to build that relationship with Him.

I already shared how prayer led me to a beautiful new relationship with Vito that brought Joy and dancing back to my life. I expected God to answer that prayer (although not the way He did). I had already established a relationship with Him and knew how He orchestrates events to answer a prayer.

Thinking back to 1989, I remember crying out to God, unsure of what to expect. Intellectually, I believed in God, but I did not have a personal relationship with Him. My marriage was a mess. I was terrified for my kids because of the bad choices Chuck and I were making. I knew the people I was hanging around didn't have my best interests in mind. I was craving positive, affirming, reciprocal relationships.

"I can't do this anymore, God! I need help. I don't know what I need or where I will find it, but I need it, God, because I'm desperate. I'm miserable. Lead me somewhere where there are Christians around. I need to be around better people."

About three weeks after I prayed that prayer, God led me to a young woman who took me to Bible Study Fellowship. That was the turning point for me. I became friends with a beautiful group of young women who met at a church, not two minutes away from my house. I didn't even know the church was there! Even during my first visit, I knew I was home. I cried, I felt loved. I got started in the scriptures and studying the Bible. I took to learning the Bible like a sponge. Let's soak up this remarkable study here, I remember thinking to myself. I was ready, so ready.

That young woman who took me to the Bible study mysteriously vanished out of my life after that. The Lord does that. He will bring people into our lives, and He will bring us into other people's lives for extraordinary purposes—His purposes. We may not understand what is happening, and then suddenly they're gone. They fade away. God led me to that Bible Study as an answer to my prayer.

Over the years, prayer has led me to different people, Bible studies, and books that I needed in my life at just the right time. Writing this book is an answer to a prayer–my prayer and, maybe, a response to your prayer.

Here is the thing that is hard to believe but is absolutely true. We do not have to be perfect to come to God in prayer. We do not have to know the Bible front to back or have the ideal words when we pray. We can be broken and messy. The prayer that led me to Bible Study Fellowship wasn't perfect. I had no idea what I needed and certainly didn't think I was hungry for the Word of God. I was not thinking of the Bible at all. I just knew I needed to change, that I wanted to change, and I prayed. I just asked God to help me and lead me to Christians, and He took it from there.

Prayer is such a powerful resource because God wants our hearts. That's all He wants. He wants our hearts. When we take that first step and seek Him through prayer, oh my goodness, does God move.

Scriptures and Music

By his divine power, God has given us everything we need for living a godly life. We have received all of this by coming to know him, the one who called us to himself by means of his marvelous glory and excellence. 2 Peter 1:3 NLT

We talk to God and pour out our souls (mind, will, and emotions) to Him through prayer. Through the Bible, His Word is essential because the Bible is God's way of talking to us. The Bible is a treasure. It is filled with over 7,000 promises, enough for Him to reach every person in their unique way, so personal to the individual. After all these years as a daily student of the Bible, I find a new promise from God every time I read it.

Yes. The Bible holds all the answers you need to start and maintain a relationship with God. It contains his love letters to you; what a fantastic treasure. Knowing the Bible helps you to get to know God well.

The Bible is the answer, but what motivates people to think about getting into reading it? Until you develop a personal relationship with God through prayer, the Bible can seem an intimidating endeavor rather than a treasure chest of promises.

I recall sitting in a hotel room in Sioux City, Iowa, back when my life was in the pits of hell. I cannot remember why I was there or how I got there. I know I was consumed with a feeling of despair and shame. I had no personal relationship with Christ yet. Still, I picked up the Gideon Bible (placed in many hotel rooms), and I just said, "Okay, I'm just going to open it and see what it says, random." I guess I was looking for lightning to strike or some sort of magic to happen. I wish I could tell you I found my life's purpose that night, but I do not even remember what I read. Something about Satan or the devil; it didn't mean that much to me at the time. I was not ready to hear what God had to say. I was like a teenager enduring through a conversation with her parents, not listening, but not 'not hearing' either. No connection.

I had to work through three years of recovery and get some stability over the insanity before I felt led to study the Bible. I was praying and talking to God, but I was still not yet ready to start absorbing the love of God and how He wants us to live a sane, Joyful life. That takes time.

I'm not sharing this rather uncomfortable story to give you a pass on digging into the Word of God. Still, I do hope I can help your journey be a bit easier than mine was. I know the Bible is off-putting at first, but it is full of God's tenderness, mercy, and devotion to us. It is God's response to the prayers that pour out of our souls (mind, will, and emotions).

Let me share another way that I immerse myself in God's Word. Since I love music and dancing, I listen to Christian music. Many contemporary Christian songs are based on scripture and combining the Word with music is a real inspiration. For example, the song "He Who Began a Good Work in Me" by Steve Green is based on Philippians 1:6. The song inspires so much energy because the music, combined with the positive scripture, is an awesome conversation with the Almighty.

Christian music comes in all different genres, so there is something for everyone. Unlike its secular counterparts, the messages in the songs are affirming and positive. If you have never listened to Christian radio, or the Christian Music section on iTunes, I encourage you to give it a try.

Studies are definitive about the effects that music has on a listener. Music can inspire, soothe, and energize. It can make you happy or comforted. By adding Christian messages to the extraordinary power of the music, the results can be miraculous. I have a friend whose husband is in end-stage cancer, and the only thing that comforts him in this phase of his life is Christian music. He cannot communicate with his wife or friends, but when she turns on the music he loves, he sings along. It is that powerful.

Prayer, scripture, and affirming Christian music all have one thing in common: They focus on the positive over the negative, the Joy over the sorrow, the healing over the sickness.

Let's be clear: I'm not suggesting you ignore the bad things in your life, but rather focus on constructive, affirming things. A few years ago, I had an awakening. I listened to a radio station in the morning that played beautiful classical music but broadcast awful news—the kind of information that spotlights the negatives to jolt the listener. Every morning I woke up to this negative input, and it was on my mind all day long. I was so heavy-hearted. I discovered K-LOVE Christian Radio (www.klove.com), available at various radio stations throughout the country and streams on the Internet. It describes itself as positive and encouraging. The station does not ignore current events, but the hosts talk about them in a proactive way–how to pray and how we can help. They play amazing Christian music. Since I have switched stations from that other, more negative station, I feel much more productive and wanting to contribute to the day.

Guard your mind, friend, because, truthfully, isn't it the most valuable asset you have? You have a choice whether to slowly get sucked into music (or news channels or books or movies) with negative impacts but believe me, that is not healthy for your mind. Allowing yourself to be filled with negativity from outside sources will certainly not bring you Joy.

Negative input will slowly crowd out the positive until your mind is so full of harmful inputs that you feel anxious and fearful all day long. Negative data has much more impact on most people than neutral or positive information or circumstances do. The negative has more power over us. That is the enemy's plan *"The thief comes only to steal and kill and destroy; [God] comes that they may have life, and have it to the full." (John 10:10 NLT).* Push those negative things away and make room for the new, positive inputs, such as prayer, music, and scripture. Avoid trying to deny reality because you cannot ignore it. It is real. Sickness and suffering are real. They can't be denied or ignored, but you can look for encouragement every day to give you hope and believe that life is good. Then watch. Be alert for how God works in positive ways in your life.

> *Finally, brothers and sisters, whatever is true, whatever is noble, whatever is right, whatever is pure, whatever is lovely, whatever is admirable— if anything is excellent or praiseworthy—think about such things. Whatever you have learned or received or heard from me, or seen in me—put it into practice. And the God of peace will be with you. Philippians 4: 8-9 NIV*

CHAPTER 6
BE WITH BELIEVERS

> *Therefore encourage one another and build each other up, just as in fact you are doing.*
> *1 Thessalonians 5:11 NIV*

I have a Facebook friend who is a breast cancer survivor. Every day she reaches out to me with lovely quotes and inspirational sayings. I so look forward to receiving those "happy shots." One day, I realized that my friend is reaching out and encouraging me every day with these inspiring snippets. She would probably like some motivation in return, so I began to reciprocate with optimistic scripture messages. It has become a volley between the two of us, and it is contagious. We encourage each other.

I have said this before, that God made us for relationships. Relationships are not merely important, they are vital to our survival. That is because God knows it's easier to get through tough times with others' help, and it is more fun to celebrate the good times surrounded by people that care.

After 45 years of marriage, I lost my soulmate, Chuck, to a heart attack. I have shared how devastated I was to be left alone suddenly. We had been friends since the seventh grade. We stuck together through the great times and some very dark and scary times during the alcoholic years. With God's intervention, we got through those rough years, and our marriage became better than ever.

When Chuck died, I knew we finished well and was so grateful to God for working in our marriage over all those years. However, it hurt to be alone. I felt adrift and abandoned.

My daughter and my grandson moved in with me right away, and that gave me people–relationships. They gave me a purpose to get up in the morning and love on Heather and my little grandson. He was so close to Chuck and missed him too. They encouraged me as I encouraged them.

One day, Heather asked, "Mom, you've got a lot of Godly girlfriends. Could we get together and start a Bible study?" She was hurting too, so I invited a bunch of friends over intending to put together a Bible study.

Well, in that first meeting, the Joy of the Lord just came over us, and we could not focus on the topic of forming a Bible study. We joked and reminisced and belly laughed. We basked in Joy, something I had not done in so long. It was clear the other women craved the same.

Finally, we conceded that God did not seem to want us to conduct just another Bible study. He knew what we needed. He wanted us to have fun and to laugh. We formed the Ladies of Laughter (LOL). We organized a theme party every month. We would get together and play and laugh, and oh, we had so many fun parties together. We were just laughing and playing. God wanted us to play.

For about two years, we allowed ourselves to suspend the weight of the world and to play. That ministered to a lot of us who were hurting. Even though they all originally came to support Heather and me, it turned out that we had so much fun—so much fun.

Bible Study Groups

The LOL group was an incredible collection of women, and just what I needed to get through my grief. Bible study groups, however, have been the backbone of my Joy from the first time I discovered Bible Study Fellowship.

Understanding the Bible on your own can be a struggle. Since God made us for a relationship, there is something special about studying the Bible with others. That first experience with Bible Study Fellowship has made me an apostle for the fantastic things that can happen through group Bible study. It can be at your local church, among a group of neighbors, or through a more formal organization such as Bible Study Fellowship.

BSF (BSFInternational.org) was initially formed as a resource for missionaries in the field who desperately needed to be fed with the Word. It is hard to evangelize and give yourself to others when your bucket is empty, so BSF was developed for the fellowship and nurturing of missionaries.

One thing led to another, and BSF expanded worldwide and opened to everyone. They review all 66 books of the Bible in a very organized manner. I attended BSF meetings once a week at a church, and at the time I joined, they were studying the Book of John. That is still my favorite book of the Bible because of what I discovered through that study. In my early 50s, I was a baptized Christian. Still, I knew nothing about inviting Jesus into my heart and then really having a personal relationship with him. I had no understanding of the Holy Spirit coming to live within me and empowering me. I had to learn about that.

I spent nine joyful years in BSF with other women who were hungry to learn God's Word. I was a sponge when I got into Bible Study Fellowship. I couldn't wait to read my notes, learn, soak up, and be more empowered by it all. The study led me to seek other ways to get close to God, and I soon found myself memorizing promises from Scripture and praying more often. I have become eager to empower other people with God's Word.

I cannot encourage you enough to find a Bible study to learn more about God's promises with people hungry to learn. To adopt the Almighty into your life, pray for an opportunity for Bible study to present itself to you. As Jesus taught: *"For where two or three gather in my name, there am I with them." (Matthew 18:20 NIV)*.

Al Anon, AA, similar recovery programs

In Chapter 4, we talked of lures many people have that mask the solution that can bring real Joy–Jesus Christ. Lures can take many forms: drug abuse, gambling, over-spending, even sex or control issues. The enemy loves to encourage our strongholds because they keep us from thinking about *"whatever is true, whatever is noble, whatever is right, whatever is pure, whatever is lovely, whatever is admirable—if anything is excellent or praiseworthy—think about such things. Whatever you have learned or received or heard from me, or seen in me—put it into practice. And the God of peace will be with you."* *(Philippians 4:8-9 NIV) (a promise).*

Covering up your destructive situation with lures will not release you from your pain. Some people go down into deep hell. It makes you crazy. You lose control emotionally all the time. I had no control over my emotions or my outbursts. Then I felt guilty for the way I was acting. The pattern is the same for any lure.

My lure was alcohol. I made terrible choices, lots of them. I knew I was doing wrong and had no clue how to stop. I did not know how to take care of what I needed to. Looking back, I realize a lot of what was holding me back from changing to a positive life direction was due to the drinking itself, both Chuck's and mine. I know I would not have made so many terrible choices if I hadn't been drinking back then, but God's grace pulled me out before it was too late. It was a lengthy recovery period. It was lonely and confusing, and the emotions were so dark. I just had to seek relief. I was led to Al-Anon, and later, to Alcoholics Anonymous.

Al-Anon and AA are recovery programs. They are the most visible programs because so many people struggle with alcohol as a lure. A quick Internet search of the phrase, "recovery program," and [your lure] and search results will likely reveal a plan designed for your personal challenge.

Recovery programs are based on surrendering to a power greater than yourself! They teach that accountability, love, and acceptance lead to spiritual growth. There are meetings where you admit your failures and encourage others to do the same. At first, the meetings are no fun at all. I remember sitting in the car in my driveway, thinking, "I don't want to go. I don't want to do this. This is crazy. It's not going to help me."

If you are in the same mindset, I encourage—no—I press you to go anyway. Apply whatever motivation you must to get you there, whether you want to or not. It was shame and embarrassment that finally got me to a meeting. I was desperate to do something to help my family and myself. We had so many shattered dreams.

At my first meeting, I thought everybody was crazy because they were laughing. I thought that's nuts. I don't get it. I'm desperate. I'm miserable, and I'm sad and scared. And these people are happy! What's that all about? The group just loved on me and assured me I was not crazy, and that they would help me. All I had to do was hang in there.

Remember, the enemy wants your lure to stay strong because when you are hooked on the negative, the enemy wins. Recovery programs are an excellent resource when you feel trapped in a devastating cycle of a stronghold, either in yourself or someone you love. They will push you to get off the merry-go-round of denial and find positive, affirmative solutions to attain your Joy.

Mentors

I have shared with you several excellent resources that have helped me in my journey for Joy through some pretty tough times. I was on my own much of the time until I discovered that Jesus is, and will always be, my ultimate mentor. I felt as though I had to search for answers myself. At first, I failed to see that God was placing opportunities and solutions in my path because I had no mentor or advisor to point out those God moments.

I long to be that mentor for you, the one that reminds you that you are not alone in your search for Joy. God yearns to guide your path and bring you all the Joy you can imagine. You do not have to start from scratch. Learn from my mistakes. Seek a recovery program if a lure plagues you. Search out a Bible study group or individual advisor to encourage you to find God's grace. Focus on positive messages, music, and Scriptures that can help you overcome the negative emotions that can consume you and steal your Joy.

I had to discover these resources, but I happily share them with you to assure you that there is hope regardless of how hopeless or dark it seems right now. You have already taken the first step by reading this book. Further help and hope await if you will just take the next step in the Lord. You will find Joy because your heart is in the right place. Your heart wants to grow and change, and taking the next step takes courage. I am proud of you for doing that. I'm so, so proud of you for taking that step. Joy is within your grasp.

Dar's Testimony

FOR REFLECTION: SECTION 2
Adopt the Almighty

- ♥ Do you ever sense that there is something/someone more significant than you?
- ♥ What did you do about it?
- ♥ Who do you know that loves you and that you can trust to ask for help?
- ♥ What if there is no one to ask?
- ♥ Are you willing to speak your thoughts/feelings out loud to yourself or to the invisible?

DAR GEIGER

TESTIMONY

BEFORE: I was born into a great family, so I thought I was a real Christian. I attended Sunday school. However, I have discovered that thinking I was a Christian and actually living as one were two different things. I thanked God for my food and said my bedtime prayers, but I never brought my true hurts or disobediences to God because I thought he would punish me. I never read the bible because I assumed it was too hard to understand.

All through my life, I tried many things to fill my inner needs. I struggled with the pain of emptiness, and had a craving in my heart for significance. Some of my negative choices were abusing alcohol and tobacco, and going on shopping sprees. I used to bring home a lot of clothes and model them for my husband, knowing full well that he would probably let me keep all of them. That was controlling, and my charge card was out of control. I needed to feel like I had some significance. Yet, my negative choices caused me pain and separation from God. I either felt guilty or empty. I thought it was up to me or my husband to take care of my needs. When I finally realized that what I was doing only made matters worse, I had judged myself as "worthless" and believed that I was going to hell because things kept getting worse.

HOW: I remember vividly the weekend of our wedding anniversary in '85. I realized how our marriage and family were literally falling apart, and there seemed to be nothing that I could do about it. I knew then that I needed God's help because I felt absolute despair. Then all of a sudden a light bulb went on in my head and I remembered that God was there for me, even if there was no one else. I just prayed a thank you to God for being there and for assurance that everything was going to be alright because --
I FINALLY GAVE THE CONTROL OVER TO GOD.

AFTER: One day I stopped at a food store that I don't normally go to, and I saw an old friend. We talked for a while. My friend invited me to join her at a Bible study, which was being held the very next day. Surprisingly, that sounded so good becuase I was so ready for the truth. The next day when I went into the church I felt like I belonged.

When I began studying the Bible, I realized how everyone has sinned, and that Christ died on the cross for all of us past, present and future. I just never understood the incredible GIFT that my Heavenly Father had given to me, nor what it all meant until I began to study His WORD, and the Holy Spirit began to bring it all alive to me.

I truly believe and have received forgiveness. I continue to confess my sin, one day at a time, and receive forgiveness, one day at a time. I'm also able to forgive others. And I know God, Jesus, my loved ones and I will be together forever because of GRACE.
(undeserved, unmerited mercy)

By Darlene Geiger, March, 2000

D.A.**N**.C.E. WITH HIM

SECTION 3–**N**urture Nearness

Come to me, all you who are weary and burdened, and I will give you rest. Take my yoke upon you and learn from me, for I am gentle and humble in heart, and you will find rest for your souls. Matthew 11: 28-29 NIV

DAR GEIGER

CHAPTER 7
NURTURING IS ACTION

Section two touched on several helpful ways to overcome injurious habits and seek Joy. Of all the suggestions, there is one underlying theme that will get you the farthest in your search for Joy. That is to nurture nearness with the ultimate Mentor–Jesus Christ. He says: *"Come to me, all you who are weary and burdened, and I will give you rest. Take my yoke upon you and learn from me, for I am gentle and humble in heart, and you will find rest for your souls" (Matthew 11: 28-29 NIV).*

Building a relationship with Christ doesn't happen overnight. Consider a toddler learning to walk. Even though she wants to walk so badly, she stumbles and falls on her butt many times before succeeding. God knows our hearts. Even when we fall on our butts, He reaches His hand toward us to help us up. It's a relationship that God never fails. Only we can be the ones to give up and fail, and our only failure in God's eyes is not trying. Nurturing a relationship requires action.

Vito

> *I can do all things through Christ who strengthens me. Philippians 4:13 NKJV*

The first time Vito called me after I met him at Anthony's, I felt brave and adventurous, agreeing to go dancing with him. I met his friends. He was such a good dancer. We had so much fun; it felt like we just clicked. When he dropped me off after our first dancing date, he stuck his head out the car window and loudly announced, in his heavy Italian accent, "Darlena, I miss you already." Charming, yes, but I was cautious. I thought, "Oh boy, is he coming on strong!"

He called me again. I'm thinking, "Okay, a little bit too aggressive." I was putting on the brakes.

But Vito persisted. Soon, we were dancing two or three times a week. My weekday schedule was full. I would make time for Vito on weekends, but I kept my weekdays and nights to myself. But over time, Vito persisted. We were so compatible that my weekend time with Vito stretched further and further into the week. And then, we fell in love. Those four years were full of Joy and laughter and great love.

Vito was 14 years older than me. I was terrified to nurture our relationship to the next level because I was fearful of losing someone close to me again. I thought that would be too painful. God finally showed me that we were a gift to each other. From that moment on, we brought comfort, and Joy and laughter to each other, and they were just the most beautiful years together.

The Lord knows your heart. He wants you to draw close, but it takes action on your part. You need to reach out to him. Make a move. Say, "I need you." Nurture your relationship with God. Once you do that, you will find great comfort. You will have Joy.

Praying is action

> *We know that anyone born of God does not continue to sin; the One who was born of God keeps them safe, and the evil one cannot harm them. 1 John 5: 18 NIV*

Vito and I had the telephone. We had our dancing dates and face to face time to talk to each other.

To nurture a relationship with God, you have prayer. Prayer is not tangible like the phone in your pocket, but it is as direct a line between you and God as all other communication methods.

Most people believe that if they do not have a relationship with God, then starting one is hard. In reality, all you have to do is pray and listen. Take that first step. If you've never reached out to talk to God, then how can you find out if He's there?

If you have lost (or never found) your Joy, and you prolong a move to do so, you're going to stagnate. I understand that trying something new can be scary. Your life might not be great, but at least it is predictable, right? What happens if you start praying to God, and things change? Or worse, what if you go out on a limb, give prayer a try, and nothing happens? Does that mean you are praying incorrectly? What are you supposed to say to God?

Trust me. Nothing feels better than when you act and make that one step in a different direction to give God a call. If you are hurting and unhappy, the worst that could happen is nothing. I assure you that God does not grade your prayers like a teacher with a thick red marker. You need no fancy language, no rehearsed speech. You don't even need to pray in full sentences. You do not have to follow a specific outline.

Let me give you God's phone number: *Jeremiah 33:3 (NIV)* *"Call to me and I will answer you and tell you great and unsearchable things you do not know."*

Just say:

"God, would you talk to me please? If You're there, let me hear You. Let me see You. I don't know You, but I want to. Please place someone in my life who can help me. I want to change. I need help."

Then God does amazing things. Pour out your heart and just speak from your soul, mind, will, and emotions. "I don't know what to do. I need help. I don't even know who You are yet, but I feel terrible. I don't like my life. Help me. Show me."

He will. God wants people's hearts. He wants you to come to Him. He loves it when people come to Him when they are hurting and when they are Joyful. God loves us and says, "Come. Just come. I am here for you. Just ask."

You may be thinking, "And then what? What do I do after I ask?"

Great question! Just like when you are talking to a friend, there comes a time where you stop talking and listen. Wait to hear from God. Expect to hear from Him.

Waiting expectantly is action

> *In the morning, I lay my requests before you and wait expectantly. Psalm 5:3 NIV*

After asking for help and a response through prayer, your next step is to wait expectantly.

It sounds too simple to be true — kind of like one of those outrageous guarantees from late-night infomercials. BUT WAIT, THERE'S MORE!!!

It is that simple. And that hard. Waiting is not easy. If you don't believe me, ask a kid on Christmas morning, staring at the clock until the pre-agreed time that they can wake up their parents. Waiting can be torture.

David knew something about praying and waiting. The author of many of the Psalms wrote of those themes repeatedly. His songs give us some insight as to how we should wait for God's reply to our prayers:

Let all that I am wait quietly before God, for my hope is in him. (Psalm 62:5 NLT)

We should wait *quietly*. When you are on the phone with a friend, do you say your piece and then jump up and turn on the TV before they have a chance to speak? No, after you have said your bit, you stop talking and wait for their reply. The same goes for your conversations with God. You cannot expect to hear His answer if, immediately after prayer, you introduce noise into your day. Be quiet and listen for God's reply.

Wait patiently for the Lord. Be brave and courageous. Yes, wait patiently for the Lord. (Psalm 27:14 NLT)

We should wait *patiently*. Today, many of us define patience as the ability to suppress our annoyance at a delay. That is undoubtedly part of what is meant by waiting patiently. God's timing is not our timing, and you will not always get an answer immediately after praying. Try to avoid getting annoyed at God for what you perceive as a delayed answer to your prayer.

Patience in the Bible, especially the New Testament, is anything but passive. In Hebrews, the author advises:

… let us lay aside every weight, and the sin which so easily ensnares us, and let us run with endurance the race that is set before us.(Hebrews 12:1 NKJV)

From this passage, we can discern that patience is not passive at all. Instead, it is the act of persevering (or enduring) as you move toward an objective. Looking at patience in this light, David's words: "wait patiently for the

Lord. Be brave and courageous," takes on a richer, more valuable meaning. This leads us to the last way David suggests in the Psalms that we should wait.

In the morning, Lord, you hear my voice; in the morning, I lay my requests before you and wait expectantly. (Psalm 5:3 NIV)

We should wait *expectantly*. Why is a child able to wait until the appointed hour on Christmas morning? When he wakes his tired parents, he will get his presents. Do you pray with the same confidence? Or are you just going through the motions, assuming you will not get an answer before you even begin? God wants us to pray and then wait, expectantly, knowing something is going to happen!

Are you starting to see that even though it may not seem so at first blush, this all takes action? To nurture a relationship with Jesus, to make a change for the better in your life, to move forward, you must make a move. Take an action step. That action comes from either your heart, your mouth, in your mind, or on your knees. To move forward rather than falling backward, you must be the one to make a move.

First, pray.

Then, wait and watch, expectantly.

Journaling your conversations and progress

I suggest you keep a prayer journal where you can record your conversations with God and the things that happen in your life. Soon you will start to see the connections between your prayers and your circumstances. A good possibility is that what you write in your prayer journal is God speaking to you about something He wants you to remember, meditate, or focus upon, all of which are further actions.

What can you "expect" from prayer?

You can expect love. I don't mean romantic love or even any kind of worldly love. God is love. I know that sounds like a cliched statement. God's love is more than we can understand, we need it more than we realize, and it is right here in front of us. We just need to ask for it. There are so many God stories of people in situations that could not be solved on their own. In His love, God put it all together into what we call a miracle if we are looking for it, or just a fortunate coincidence if we are not. The Bible says, *"And we know that in all things God works for the good of those who love Him." (Romans 8:28 NIV)*. When we love someone, we trust them, and God wants you to trust Him.

That is why I suggest you keep a prayer journal, so you can see God working in your life over time; so you can find those God moments and know that He is working toward your well-being. It isn't just luck or isolated incidents that don't connect. Most of the time, when we have trouble nurturing nearness through prayer, it is due to our stubbornness. We want to be in control of things, not give our will to God. We want to make things happen. If it were that easy, though, you would already have all the Joy you need in life. You need to accept that you cannot do it by yourself. Maybe you need to try another prayer, such as, "God, help me get over myself because I've been trying to run everything on my own, but nothing's working. Help me get over myself and remove what's blocking me from seeing the truth."

Sometimes we are looking so hard for an answer to prayer that we overlook all the work God is doing in our lives. There are times when you need to get your mind off the problem and trust that things will work out without you obsessing over it. Play some music, go dance, or call a friend. Read a book. Do whatever you can do to free yourself from anxious thoughts. Trust in a solution more incredible than you. What a relief to learn you are not permanently stuck with your toxic thoughts. You can change your thoughts. You can replace them with other, more empowering ideas and words. Positive, encouraging, life-giving words and thoughts are so important, and God's Word is full of His promises that He loves you and will care for you. You do not have to solve your problems on your own. You do not have to worry all day long to make the problems go away. "Fix your thoughts on what is true, honorable, right, pure, lovely, and admirable. Think about things that are excellent and worthy of praise" (Philippians 4:8 NLT).

The sunflower exactly symbolizes how I want my relationship with Jesus to be. It represents happiness and optimism with its bright and cheerful coloring and shape. Here is a little-known fact about sunflowers—they always follow the sun. Before dawn breaks, the sunflower faces east, toward the sunrise. As the sun moves from east to west, the sunflower turns westward as well. When the sun sets, the flower reverts to its original position facing east to begin the cycle anew the next day. Just like the sunflower trusts the sun, I encourage you to follow the SON. When things are good, look to God with thanksgiving. When things get dark, ask for encouragement in the Lord, and He will give you the strength you need to get through.

DAR GEIGER

CHAPTER 8
FACING THE ENEMY

Nurturing nearness with God through prayer and expectant watching and waiting is possibly the most powerful tool you have for overcoming your strongholds. Therefore, the enemy works hard to find ways to impede that relationship. Here are two common ploys the enemy uses:

1. He tries to convince you that God is not answering your prayers, and, therefore, must not care about you.

   God always answers prayers, but it might not be the answer you want or expect. He answers in one of three ways: yes, no, and wait. We want the "yes" answer, and we want it now. A "no" or "wait" answer often feels like no answer.

   It comes down to trust. Do you trust God or the enemy? The Bible tells you what is in both of their hearts: *"The thief comes only to steal and kill and destroy. I came that they may have life and have it abundantly" (John 10:10 ESV)*. So which will it be? A relationship with someone who loves you and wants the best for you, or putting your trust in an antagonist who wants to kill and destroy your Joy?

2. The enemy confuses you into not knowing if God is helping you choose between two options or if you are merely picking the choice you want.

    I would suggest that when you are confused over two choices, you are likely rushing the answer. God wants us to have FAITH, which is a "Fantastic Adventure In Trusting Him." We don't always get answers immediately. I prayed about whether I should write this book, and God's answer came to me over time. Sometimes, I get immediate feedback, and I know in my spirit how to proceed. Fast answers to questions and decisions will come to you too as you nurture nearness with Christ. Sometimes, however, you must wait. It is a journey of trust.

We don't always feel like an answer is received

Unfortunately, the enemy is highly skilled at twisting our thoughts into knots. If you are facing an important decision and pray about it, for example, you might be unable to predict the answer. It is a journey, a personal journey, and all I can do is encourage you to be courageous and curious enough to give it some blind TRUST. "**T**ry **R**elying **U**pon the **S**avior's **T**ruth."

When the enemy starts to discourage me, I turn to another acronym that God gave me to re-focus my mind away from the enemy and toward the Lord. That acronym is BELIEVE:

B–BLESSED

E–EVERY DAY

L–by the LORD'S

I–INCREASE of

E–EMPOWERMENT for

V–VICTORY and

E–ENERGY

Blessed every day by the Lord's increase of empowerment for victory and energy. I have a sign on my refrigerator that says, "Believe all things are possible." Every time I see it, I engage in a little spiritual warfare by dancing around my kitchen. While dancing, I pray that I (and others) will be blessed every day by the Lord's increase of empowerment for victory and energy!

He is the hand. I am the glove. I can't do anything without him, but *"I can do all this through Him who gives me strength."* (*Philippians 4:13 NIV*). Yes, God. Thank you, thank you, thank you! I am blessed every day by the Lord's increase of empowerment for victory and energy!

Be patient

> *Do not be anxious about anything, but in every situation, by prayer and petition, with thanksgiving, present your requests to God.*
> *Philippians 4:6 NIV*

Through enduring the COVID-19 pandemic over the past year, I have learned so much about patience and forfeiting my control to God. I have learned that nothing gets done of my own power. He is the hand, and I am the glove— just the messenger, not the message.

We cannot change anybody. Only God can do that. You can be a conduit, through prayer and nurturing with love. Christ is the vine, you are the branch. It is God's progress and His timing. We just have to trust Him and do our part, and then leave the rest in His hands.

Our stubborn desire to control the timing and results of our prayers makes patience so hard. And boy, sometimes patience is hard. Look at the Israelites. They were stubborn and wanted things to go their way and by their timing. As a result, they wandered in the desert for 40 years on a trip that should have taken them 11 days. God felt it was important for them to learn about patience, faith, and trust. It's a huge risk to take a step of faith and say, "Okay. I don't feel it. I don't see it. I don't understand it. But I'm taking that first step just like a baby does when they're first learning to walk."

> *You too, be patient and stand firm,*
> *because the Lord's coming is near.*
> *James 5: 8 NIV*

DAR GEIGER

CHAPTER 9
REPLACE NEGATIVE THOUGHTS
WITH POSITIVE THOUGHTS

It is easy to dwell on the bad things in life over the good. With the COVID-19 pandemic and adverse effects on our economy, it is safe to say we have all had some anxious moments these last few months. The enemy works on each of us uniquely to lure us from seeing the positive to focusing on the negative. He knows how to make us feel downtrodden and abandoned. Even if you are on to his ploys, you might have trouble turning away from the enemy's tricks.

Gratitude

> *Always be joyful. Never stop praying. Be thankful in all circumstances, for this is God's will for you who belong to Christ Jesus.*
>
> *1 Thessalonians 5: 16-18 NLT*

I believe one of the most effective ways to cast out the enemy's influence is to practice gratitude. When I first entered Al-Anon, I was so sad and in so much mental pain that I wanted to end my life. My Al-Anon sponsor helped me through that dark time in my life by helping me to understand how important it is to be grateful. I'll never forget one conversation we had when I felt as though my life was in the pits of hell.

My sponsor asked me to tell her just a few things I was grateful for, despite my present circumstances.

"I can't even think of one thing," I told her. That is how miserable I was.

"Okay," she replied, "let's do a reality check here. Did you get out of bed this morning? Did you put your feet on the floor?"

Sullenly, I answered, "yessss…."

"Are you talking to me right now? Are you drinking that cup of coffee? Do you have a family you love?"

On and on, she fired off things that I could be grateful for despite my circumstances, all of which I had taken for granted, preferring to wallow in misery.

Gratitude is huge…Huge! Take a look at the things you have not appreciated in your life that are really great. Consider setting aside a place in your prayer journal for gratitude lists that can help you feel better when you are low. Maybe even incorporate your gratitude lists into your daily prayer sessions. What a fantastic way to ward off the enemy and find your Joy again.

Follow Your Heart to remain positive

In the book of Ruth, Naomi moved from Bethlehem to Moab with her husband and two sons to escape a famine. Her sons married Moabite women, Ruth and Orpah. Over the next several years, Naomi's husband and both sons died, leaving Naomi, Ruth, and Orpah alone. The widow Naomi decided to return to her home in Bethlehem to grow old amongst her family. However, before she left, she spoke with Ruth and Orpah, telling them they should stay in Moab and remarry. Orpah agreed.

Ruth, however, was not persuaded. Naomi was family! Not only that, but she was also a dear friend.

"Don't ask me to leave you and turn back. Wherever you go, I will go; wherever you live, I will live. Your people will be my people, and your God will be my God. Wherever you die, I will die, and there I will be buried. May the Lord punish me severely if I allow anything but death to separate us!" (Ruth 1: 16-17 NLT).

With that famous speech, Ruth followed Naomi. Naomi did not force her. She was grieving and had lost her husband and sons. All she had was her beloved daughters-in-law. Naomi wanted what she thought was best for them, remaining in Moab and remarrying there. Ruth had a choice and decided she would stick with Naomi and be there for her through her grief.

Ruth taught me to follow your heart. Her husband died too. She was grieving also, but she did not let that stop her from seeing the possibilities before her. It did not stop her from giving love to others.

In Bethlehem, Naomi and Ruth have a tough time. Naomi languishes in her grief, and Ruth is forced to glean food in the barley fields. The owner of one field, Boaz, notices how kind Ruth is to Naomi, taking care of her the best that she can. He takes a liking to Ruth and gives her gleaning privileges to make her life more comfortable. Ruth is fond of Boaz too. Through a series of "coincidences," they end up together and have a son, Obed, who becomes the grandfather of King David, and, therefore, an ancestor of Jesus Christ.

By listening for God's direction and following His gentle prompts on her heart, Ruth, a Moabite, became part of Jesus' ancestry. Coincidence? Or was God working in her life?

Ruth could have been angry before God started working in her life. She did not have a lot going for her. Ruth had no significance in human terms. She was a poor widow who had to feed herself and her mother-in-law by picking up the small clusters of barley rejected by the field workers harvesting the crop. But Ruth stayed cheerful and happy and willing to serve. God saw into her heart and blessed her. What Joy!

Don't be childish–be childlike

My Life Scripture!
Anyone who belongs to Christ has become a new person. The old life is gone; a new life has begun! 2 Corinthians 5: 17 NLT

Having Vito in my life was such a blessing to me. Joy returned to my life after my husband's death, and I think it is because we were both willing to be childlike again. We were starting a new relationship and, at our *advanced age*, acted like little kids with crushes. Just being together permitted us to play again.

The Hy-Vee grocery store was one of our favorite playgrounds. Any little thing was so much fun. Remember what that was like as a kid? I would push the cart and give him silent signals which way to turn or stop or go. He would get so mixed up, and we would laugh out loud — silly, but so much fun.

Vito's Italian accent was so entertaining. One day we were grocery shopping at the Hy-Vee, and I asked him to help me find Crème Brule for my coffee in the dairy section. We separated slightly, looking for the Crème Brule and I hear Vito cry out, *"Hey! Kimberly!"* I turned toward him and said, "Where? Kimberly, who?"

"Nah, Nah, not Kimberly…Kimberly."

Vito's pointing into the dairy products, and when I went to look, there is the Crème Brule. His accent made it sound like Kimberly.

As comprehension came over me, I looked at him and just started belly-laughing. In my best Italian accent (which is okay, at best), I said, *"Ohhhh, Kimberly Ah Ha! Okey Dokey!"*

Other shoppers were cracking up laughing because we were having so much fun.

Vito was such a blessing! A lot of Joy!

Jesus wants you to have the Joy that comes with being young at heart. Be playful and laugh at yourself.

> *Jesus said, "Let the little children come to me, and do not hinder them, for the kingdom of heaven belongs to such as these."*
> *Matthew 19:14 NIV*

Make room for Jesus in your day

Clearly, the key to finding your Joy is to build a close, personal, joy-filled relationship with Jesus through prayer, expectant waiting, patience, and constructive, positive thinking. Still, so many people struggle to develop such a relationship.

I wrestled with the same problems. I always had hundreds of things on my mind, something to do each day that crowded out the time I needed to get close to Jesus. I would rush through my prayer time. Rather than wait patiently to hear God's reply, I would hop out of my seat to get to the next task at hand.

One day, I was attending a Bible Study class. The teacher gave me an illustration that has stuck with me and changed how I approach a relationship with Jesus.

The teacher presented us with an empty jar, explaining that the jar represents our day.

She then showed us two materials, sugar and walnuts. She told us that the sugar represents the hundreds or even thousands of things we must do or think about during the day. The walnuts represent the time we spend with Jesus.

The teacher then poured the sugar in the jar. After the jar was nearly full to the brim, she added the walnuts. Only two or three walnuts fit in the jar. She explained it demonstrates that when you prioritize the things you need to do and think about all day long, there is not much time left to give to your relationship with God. Then, the teacher dumped out the jar and started over. This time, she put the walnuts in the jar first then poured in the sugar. Amazingly, both the walnuts and the sugar fit with room to spare.

The teacher's point became crystal clear to me. When God is first, everything else will fall into place. Every time you take quiet time to pray and listen to God, every time you wake up saying, "thank you for this day, God, I'm trusting You today," is another walnut of time in the jar. Everything will change after that!

Don't worry; there will still be room for the hundreds or thousands of things you need to do. By surrendering your heart first thing in the morning, other tasks and demands in your schedule will more easily fall into place. That doesn't mean everything will always go your way. The enemy is still at work in the world. However, I assure you that when you put Jesus first, the Joy found in Him will be there in good times and bad. Your time with Jesus will be something you reach for, even look forward to, all day long. Your first thought in the morning is Jesus, and your last thought at night is Jesus. Thank you, Jesus, for this Joyful day!

FOR REFLECTION: SECTION 3
Nurture Nearness

Questions:

- ♥ Who/What makes you feel "nurtured"? (protected, supported, comforted, encouraged).
- ♥ How can we tell when we're running on empty?
- ♥ What if we wait too long? Can it be detrimental?
- ♥ Are you a martyr? Humility doesn't mean we think less of ourselves–we simply learn to think of ourselves less.
- ♥ Can you find anything to be grateful for?

DAR GEIGER

D.A.N.**C**.E. WITH HIM

SECTION 4–**C**onnect to Christ

And we know that in all things God works for the good of those who love him, who have been called according to his purpose. Romans 8: 28 NIV

DAR GEIGER

CHAPTER 10
WHY CONNECT?

I have a jar of walnuts and sugar on a shelf in my sunroom to remind me to make my connection with Christ a priority in my life. That reminder has helped shape my daily routine to: *"Fix [my] thoughts on what is true, and honorable, and right, and pure, and lovely, and admirable. To think about things that are excellent and worthy of praise." (Philippians 4:8 NLT).*

I wake up to Christian radio because it is positive and encourages me to keep my mind fixed on what is lovely and admirable. I dance around my ranch home, which brings me Joy and gives me a good workout that builds endorphins and increases positivity to make me feel better. I try to keep my mind clear of negative input. That can be hard sometimes as I like to go straight to Facebook and see what is up with all my friends. Instead, I go out to my sunroom (my favorite room in the house) refreshed, and ready to talk to Jesus. That is my time to journal, pray, and look up scripture.

Connecting with Christ and growing your relationship with Him is a discipline, and no one can do it perfectly. How I connect with Him will be different than how you connect. God makes everyone unique. Some, like myself, are connectors and people-focused; others are more introverted. Whatever your temperament and personality, recognize it as a gift from God. It is not a set structure you are going for, but a mindset where you put Jesus first so that you can best use your gifts and talents to bring the Joy of the Lord to others.

Stages of a relationship

As mentioned earlier, I met my husband, Chuck, when I was in seventh grade. My family moved from Chicago to a new suburb called Schiller Park, IL. My new school tried to place me in sixth grade to align with my age, but I didn't want to do that because I had already taken sixth grade in Chicago. They allowed me to try seventh grade, and on my first day, they sat me in front of Chuck. God meant it to be!

Meet/Flirt

I was 11, and Chuck had just turned 13 when we met. The first thing he did was pull my pigtails, and I turned to him and said: "Stop that!" Chuck said that was when his heart started beating wildly, and he knew it was meant to be. It was adorable.

Nevertheless, Chuck was very shy, and even at that young age, I had an outgoing personality. I liked him, and I wanted him to like me. So, I started in on a little flirting in the schoolyard and at the local snack shop where kids would hang out after school. My girlfriends tried to intercede, and Chuck's friends encouraged him. The snack shop had a jukebox, and *"Sincerely"* by the McGuire Sisters became our unofficial song.

Be watchful for tiny, coincidental events to be placed in front of you that you will start to recognize as being delivered by God. Think of those occurrences as God flirting with you to bring you closer to Him. And, hey, you can do some flirting of your own with Him too!

Get to know each other/Find commonalities

Chuck and I soon found we were walking home together and spending time in the field near my house. There was a big tree and a stream there, and we talked nonstop and got to know each other. One day, we were at the snack shop, and he took me outside in the back, away from our friends. He just looked at me and said, "here," and handed me a ring. That's all he said. I replied, "thanks." We were going steady, I guess.

As you make more and more room in your life for Jesus, and less on worldly concerns, you will become closer. You will find yourself yearning to spend time with Him, reading scripture, personalizing it, and praying about everything. You will be searching, always looking for ways to get closer to Him.

You know what you know/Your time is all theirs

Chuck and I blossomed from there. Thinking back, we were just so cute. Chuck would ride his bike to my house and back home again nearly every day, regardless of the weather. Just like the mailman, rain, sleet, or snow, there was Chuck. My schedule altered completely. It was all about Chuck from then on. I told my mom that I was in love with him. She told me it was just puppy love. By eighth grade, however, I was even more in love with him, and he was my whole life. He was the valedictorian of the eighth-grade class and on the basketball team, and I was his cheerleader. My cheer: *"with a dig-dig-dig and a hoy, hoy, hoy— cheer for Freddy, he is our boy!"* Freddy was Chuck's name until he went to college and he changed his name to Chuck. I didn't know he was going to do this. You can imagine my surprise when I received his first letter to me!

When we were in eighth grade, I danced with another boy, and Chuck was distraught because he had not yet learned how to dance. I told him that I loved to dance, and I did not know if I wanted to date him if he could not. He instantly agreed to learn. We spent hours in the basement, and I would teach him the jitterbug and slow dancing. We became outstanding dancers, and we won a dance contest on our honeymoon. When we got married, we moved to Champagne, Illinois, and lived there for almost three years. I worked, and he went to college to get his mechanical engineering degree. My whole life was about Chuck. From the seventh grade on, we spent as much time together as we could.

If you want to pursue Joy by connecting with Christ, then be ready to change your lifestyle. That is going to take time and commitment.

There are no promises that your relationship with God will be easy

Both of Chuck's parents were alcoholics, and unfortunately, he inherited the disease. Early in our marriage, I went through the crisis of seeing the love of my life change from Jekyll into Hyde because of alcohol.

It started innocently enough. As young newlyweds, we did a lot of partying and drinking while we lived in Champagne. Looking back, I see we both made a lot of bad choices back then. After the birth of Chuck, Jr., we moved to Omaha, where Heather was born. Everything seemed to fall apart. I missed my family. Chuck's job became demanding and he started traveling a lot. The stress got to him, and he began drinking more and more. I was alone a lot when he traveled, and when he was home, he could not be there for us emotionally. Instead, he tried to buy us off with possessions, but he became unreliable as his alcohol dependency progressed. You couldn't trust his word. It was harrowing for the kids and me. I was desperate.

I finally told Chuck that I wanted to leave him. I still loved him, but I could not take it anymore. In response to the anxiety, I had started drinking again and making bad choices, and it was just tumultuous.

Telling Chuck I wanted out was God's catalyst for change in our lives. Chuck went for help first. He asked me to support him, and I agreed. He joined AA and started his recovery. I followed, first joining Al-Anon and then AA. Finally, I was led to Bible Study Fellowship.

In this world, we're going to have trials. Connecting with Christ isn't a promise that life is going to be easy. Jesus said, "Here on earth you will have many trials and sorrows. But take heart, because I have overcome the world." (John 16:33 NLT).

One day at a time

The rest of the story is all about us finding God and His Joy one day at a time. I see God as the reason why our marriage stayed intact. Although we had followed God before we wed, we strayed. It was terrible for quite some time. Dangerous, even. God poured His grace on us, intervened in our lives, and healed us, leading us to AA, Al-Anon, and BSF. We've done a lot of recovery work, and the spiritual AA program was a gift from God for both of us.

If you knew what you might have to face tomorrow, you would probably not be able to handle it. You don't have to worry about what will happen tomorrow or the day after that with God. Simply focus on the present, because it is a gift. If you keep your eyes on Him, He will guide you one day at a time to Joy in the Lord.

> *Then Jesus said, "Come to me, all of you who are weary and carry heavy burdens, and I will give you rest. Take my yoke upon you. Let me teach you because I am humble and gentle at heart, and you will find rest for your souls. For my yoke is easy to bear, and the burden I give you is light." Matthew 11: 28-30 NLT*

The enemy hates when you connect

The enemy does not want you to connect with Christ. The closer you come to developing a relationship with Jesus, the harder internal or external forces will work to pull you away from that relationship. The enemy thrives on placing roadblocks in your way and then leading you to believe you only have yourself to depend on to handle your problems. Then, he tries to keep you emotionally down and angry. At the same time, the enemy urges you to suppress those feelings to the point where you can't even recognize your grief. By the time he is through with you, you are a writhing mess.

> **The thief's purpose is to steal and kill and destroy. My purpose is to give them a rich and satisfying life. John 10:10 NLT**

If the devil thinks you're on track for doing something good for the Lord, trust me, you will experience adversity and challenges. There is no doubt about that.

I urge you to be aware of Satan's ploys. Everything begins with our thoughts. Proverbs tells us: *"A cheerful heart is good medicine, but a broken spirit saps a person's strength" (Proverbs 17:22 NLT)*. Guess what the enemy tries to do with your spirit? He tries to shatter it.

Feed your mind with good stuff to prepare you for when the enemy strikes. Peter tells us to *"Stay alert! Watch out for your great enemy, the devil. He prowls around like a roaring lion, looking for someone to devour." (1 Peter 5: 8 NLT)*. How do you feed your mind? With everything we have been working on to connect with Christ: prayer, studying God's word, waiting expectantly, serving others, and sharing your Joy. God's grace comes through faith, and faith is a choice. Choose Jesus over the enemy's tricks, and you will be filled with the fruits of the spirit. It is not all on your back. It is not all your responsibility. How wonderful! How freeing! That means you can have Joy, despite what the enemy wants to lead you to believe.

Beware of the dogs! Beware of the evil workers! Beware of the mutilators! Philippians 3:2 ISV

CHAPTER 11
WAYS TO CONNECT
WITH CHRIST

Can I give you step by step instructions on how to connect with Christ? I don't think so. Relationships are exclusive and depend on what you are going through personally and where you are in your spiritual journey. A lot of it is God's supernatural intervention. His love is hard to describe. I can share my story, but in the end, your account will be different.

I do suggest you take out your prayer journal and do two things.

First, identify your values. Values are the principles that give your life meaning and allow you to persevere through adversity. If you have been working through this book with me, you should have a good idea by now of what is essential to acquiring Joy and maintaining it throughout your life. This is not what society, culture, movies, television commercials or the news media tell you should be important, but what is necessary for you to feel true Joy. What are your values? Spend some time praying about it and understanding your values.

Next, evaluate your lifestyle. To be true to the things you value, will you have to make some changes?

Ask God to help you change what you can control and accept the things you cannot. This instruction comes from the Serenity Prayer used in recovery programs but is an appropriate meditation for anyone seeking to connect with Christ

> *God grant me the serenity to accept the things I cannot change…courage to change what I can…and wisdom to know the difference.*

Your starting point should always be prayer. Ask God to lead you. Ask Him for help and awareness, then wait, and watch, expectantly. God will reveal the resources you need to build a stronger relationship. Perhaps it will be one of the ideas suggested in Section two. Maybe it will be something different altogether. God wants a connection and knows what you need. Living your life in an active state of Joy is about seeking God and asking Him to guide you.

Trust to be vulnerable

In my early years of recovery, I would attend women's retreats through Bible Study Fellowship and Al-Anon. Those retreats taught me how important it is to trust people and be willing to be vulnerable. At first, I was not ready to open-up. I was scared to reveal truths about myself because I feared rejection. I was even terrified to be seen without makeup because I felt unprotected. The other women encouraged me to trust them and were so loving and affirmative. They taught me how to be vulnerable, and that was when I finally started to find my Joy.

Even when we are at our most vulnerable moment, we can experience the connection with God and others that He made us for. Nevertheless, when we are most vulnerable is also when we can get hurt the most.

A common deception of the enemy is to make us believe that vulnerability is a weakness. Being vulnerable can indeed hurt you, but getting hurt doesn't mean you are weak. In fact, it is often through our most vulnerable times that we grow the most. Taking the risk to expose yourself provides essential insights and lessons that lead to the intimate connections with God and others that we crave.

Look for mentors

Esther was a Jewish orphan, raised by her cousin, Mordecai, while Israel was held captive in Persia. As described in the Book of Esther, she was chosen for the King's harem, and eventually, as his wife. Esther was an ordinary woman and part of a minority race held in low esteem before this happened. In fact, the Jews were thought so lowly that when Esther was chosen for the King's harem, she kept her nationality a secret at Mordecai's urging.

When Esther became Queen, Mordecai uncovered a plot to kill the King. A discerning, God-fearing man, he told Esther about the conspiracy, and she was able to warn the King in time to thwart the assassination. Both Esther and Mordecai were rewarded for that.

More treachery was afoot, however. A few years later, Mordecai had a run-in with a court official, Haman, who Mordecai discovered was plotting to annihilate the Jews. He asked Esther to implore the King to step in and stop the scheme. Esther was afraid to do it. Who wouldn't be? First, she had hidden her identity as a Jew. Second, the penalty for going to the King's inner court uninvited if the King disapproved of your appeal, was death (yes, even for the Queen).

Mordecai counseled Esther to put aside her fear, helping her to realize that this was the very reason God chose her to be Queen. Mordecai advised:

"If you keep silent at this time, relief and deliverance will rise for the Jews from another place, but you and your father's house will perish. And who knows whether you have not come to the kingdom for such a time as this" (Esther 4:14 ESV).

Mordecai's counsel made Esther realize that she had not been chosen as the Queen merely to make her life more comfortable. God had another plan in mind. Rather than rush into the King's court demanding justice for the Jews, however, she took time to pray, fast, wait, and watch expectantly for how God wanted her to approach the King.

In the meantime, God was already at work. God gave the King insomnia. That made him call his staff to bring his book of records, probably hoping the tedium of reviewing court proceedings would put him to sleep. Instead, near dawn, he was reminded through the records how Mordecai had a hand in saving his life.

Before Esther even had a chance to go to the King and reveal Haman's conspiracy against the Jews, Haman (boo, hiss) arrived, confident that the King would approve his plot. Instead, the King, glowing from his appreciation for being alive, rules in favor of Mordecai and the Jews and permanently sent the evil Haman away.

What a great story! There are so many life lessons we can learn. It teaches that God has a plan for each of us. Everyone, ordinary as we may be, has opportunities to alter circumstances if we are courageous and willing.

The message I want to underscore here is how big a role mentoring plays in carrying out God's plan for your life. Mordecai mentored Esther, who later mentored the King, which led to saving the entire Jewish nation.

> **Walk with the wise and become wise; associate with fools and get in trouble. Proverbs 13:20 NLT**

My first mentor was my precious friend, Anne, who I met when I first started Al-Anon. She became my sponsor and took me under her wing. In addition to teaching me about being honest and vulnerable and dealing with a crisis, she became my best friend. Sponsors in recovery programs struggle with their own demons, even while reaching out to help and mentor others. Through Anne's selfless coaching, I learned that I did not need to be perfect myself to touch and help others. We had an excellent, wonderful relationship, and through Anne, I knew what it meant to be mentored as well as how to mentor others.

Fast forward 40 years, and although I have acted as a mentor to many since that first experience with Anne, I still seek out and use the wise counsel of mentors. I found my latest mentor, Dr. Rachel Smartt, by watching a video on Facebook. She was talking about her book, ***Modern Day Miracles: A Mother/Daughter Journey of Faith and Resiliency***. When I heard her, it felt like she was speaking directly to me. She was so encouraging and got me dreaming again about what I want to do with my life.

I was so inspired by her (and I think the Holy Spirit was poking at my heart to act) that I tracked her down through her website and saw that she offered a free consultation. I reached out to share a bit about myself, and we just clicked. It turns out that although we have an 18-year age difference, we have so much in common. We are both believers. She lost her husband to cancer early in their marriage and faced the challenge of raising four little girls on her own. Even so, she is positive and forward-thinking rather than dwelling on the disappointments.

Dr. Rachel is an amazing listener and has helped me clarify what is important to me and my goals and aspirations for the next chapter in my life. She gave me homework and activities to gain clarity. Even more importantly, she prayed for me, and we have prayed together. She has become a hero in my life.

> *Two people are better off than one, for they can help each other succeed. If one person falls, the other can reach out and help. But someone who falls alone is in real trouble.*
> *Ecclesiastes 4: 9-10 NLT*

Why are mentors so important? There are several reasons:

- God created you to be in relationship with others. He did not intend us to go it alone. We all need someone who can help point the way and provide stability when we are feeling off-kilter. The best way for this to happen is in the context of a relationship.
- Everyone needs accountability. That is the foundation of recovery programs such as AA and Al-Anon and is equally important in other circumstances. A mentor will help you stay true to your values and goals.
- There is always room for improvement. Even when you reach the point of coaching and advising others, you still have room to grow. Seeking out mentors throughout your life helps you stay lively and open to what God has in store for you next. It is essential throughout life to both lead and to follow.

> *Jesus replied, "You must love the Lord your God with all your heart, all your soul, and all your mind.' This is the first and greatest commandment. A second is equally important: 'Love your neighbor as yourself.' The entire law and all the demands of the prophets are based on these two commandments."*
> *Matthew 22: 37-40 NLT*

The best mentor you will ever have is the Lord. By mentoring the disciples, Jesus shared knowledge and values through His words and actions; by showing rather than telling. He demonstrated how He wanted them to act by first doing it Himself. The disciples learned through Jesus' example that God's values are different than the values of the world. He taught them to be servants to others. Finally, Jesus was not satisfied to keep it to themselves. He urged His disciples to go out into the world and practice mentoring others by building new relationships. Through His mentorship, the entire Christian religion spread and continues to expand across the globe.

The final lesson on mentoring that we get from Jesus is that it is all about heart. That's it. You do not have to be a perfectionist do-gooder or Bible thumper. That was not Jesus' example at all. He had such an extraordinary way of connecting with different personalities and getting people to think for themselves by telling parables. He mentored through love, which brought Joy to so many people.

> *For I hold you by your right hand—I, the Lord your God. And I say to you, 'Don't be afraid. I am here to help you.' Isaiah 41:13 NLT*

Be Brave to change

> *"Be strong and courageous! Do not be afraid or discouraged. For the Lord your God is with you wherever you go." Joshua 1:9 NLT*

It may seem a contradictory statement but finding your Joy can be scary. Think about it. If you are not joyful in this moment of time, you are looking to change in order to discover that Joy. It can be easy to feel overwhelmed and uncertain in those times. It can be hard to be brave enough to make the change.

As I will get into further in Chapter 12, I started my own business as a Juice Plus representative in 2002. When Vito died suddenly in June of 2018, my passion for wanting to build my Juice Plus business dimmed. I still wanted to help families thrive physically and strengthen their immunities. However, I lost interest in the organizational end of things and training new distributors. When the company offered to buy out my downline, I agreed. I still share the product and interact with my Juice Plus family, but I chose to give up the business part.

Suddenly, I found myself with a lot more time. What now? I prayed. I know there is more for me to do. What do you have for me now, Lord? Truthfully, the thought of change was terrifying.

Sometimes (a lot of times), being brave looks like stepping out of your comfort zone. If you are battling a lure like dependence, imagining life without your crutch is downright scary. Even a positive life change that takes you away from your safe zone is intimidating. No matter what you face, giving up the old and facing a new chapter in your life, regardless of how much you want it, is terrifying.

Other times, being brave means staying where you are. Back when Chuck and I struggled with alcoholism in our marriage, I wanted to haul butt and get out of there. He asked me to stay and support him, and it took all my courage to agree. Sometimes you cannot solve a problem by changing your circumstances, but rather by staying put and working for change where you are.

No one's bravery looks the same. You may be facing decisions over finances, education, career, or dealing with a toxic relationship with a family member or friend. Maybe you fear public speaking or commitment that is holding you back from your goals or dreams. Perhaps you are struggling with forgiveness or tend to blame others rather than take responsibility for your circumstances. Whatever it is that you must face, your challenges are different from battles and temptations others are going through.

To be brave means having trust in God. There are countless scriptures where the Lord advises us not to be afraid because He is with us. He doesn't suggest being brave requires us to be strong or talented or wise. No. God quiets our anxiety with the assurance that He is in control. When you hear God's nudge to be brave, rest in the certainty that He will make it work. It may not be what you expect, and it quite possibly won't be easy. Nevertheless, you will find your Joy when you trust in God to lead you there.

> **Do not be afraid, for I am with you and will bless you. Genesis 26:24 NLT**

My prayers eventually led to my meeting with Dr. Rachel. I shared with her that even though I was closing the door on a chapter in my life by selling my Juice Plus business, I did not want to formally retire. I wanted my future to be meaningful. I felt that God still had plans for me, but I didn't know what they were.

Through Rachel's mentorship, I came to realize that I craved helping other women. Over the years, I have led countless Bible study groups and shared so many beautiful memories with the women God has placed in my life. Still, my heart was crying out to help even more people find their Joy. Dr. Rachel was the one to suggest I might have a book in me. She advised, "Why don't you pray about it?" She prayed for me, as well.

Through meditation and prayer, I believe God said: "Darlene, I want you to write your story - it will be 'our book,' and it will bring glory to Me, and will bless many. *Whether you turn to the right or to the left, your ears will hear a voice behind you, saying, "This is the way; walk in it' (Isaiah 30:21 NIV).*

I see God's hand in the whole adventure. I am blessed to share my experiences and observations with more women than I could ever reach through a Bible study or small group. It has not come without a good deal of anxiety and fear along the way. I was definitely stepping out of my comfort zone when I decided to write a book. I learned that God's promises were true. He has been with me all along the way, putting just the right people in my path and handling the entire process.

Be brave in God's promises. He knows what you need to find your Joy. No matter how terrifying the change you face is, take courage in His love and assurance.

> *Do not be afraid as you go out to fight your enemies today! Do not lose heart or panic or tremble before them. For the Lord your God is going with you! He will fight for you against your enemies, and he will give you victory!*
> *Deuteronomy 20:3-4 NLT*

1959

SENIOR NOTABLE, Cutest Couple
Darlene Carlson and Fred Geiger

FOR REFLECTION: SECTION 4
Nurture Nearness

Questions:

- ♥ What does it take to have a meaningful relationship?
- ♥ Who do you want to connect with? Why?
- ♥ Does the other person have to reach out to you first? Or…are you willing to take the initiative?
- ♥ Who have your mentors been throughout your life?
- ♥ How do you bring value to others and the world?
- ♥ What does being vulnerable mean to you, and what can be the result?

DAR GEIGER

D.A.N.C.**E**. WITH HIM

SECTION 5–**E**mpower Everyone

I tell you the truth, anyone who believes in me will do the same works I have done, and even greater works, because I am going to be with the Father. John 14:12 NLT

DAR GEIGER

CHAPTER 12
IF YOU WANT TO
HELP YOURSELF,
HELP SOMEONE ELSE

My Life Scripture!
This means that anyone who belongs to Christ has become a new person. The old life is gone; a new life has begun! 2 Corinthians 5:17 NLT

Your entire journey to find Joy has focused so far on replacing your lures with the strong arm of the Lord, on replacing self-will with God's will, on replacing the enemy's control with the Lord's gentle love.

My journey to Joy has led me to understand that Joy is not something I can devise through external stimuli. No amount of alcohol, control, spending, or (name your particular lure) will bring you Joy.

Joy comes from within because God created us with Joy already hardwired in. *"The Joy of the Lord is your strength" (Nehemiah 8:10 NLT)!*

Let's explore the backstory of that scripture for a moment. The Israelites had just been freed from captivity and returned to Jerusalem. They were their own nation again. The governor, Nehemiah, ordered all citizens old enough to understand to hear a reading of the traditional Jewish law.

As Ezra, the priest, read the law, the citizens began weeping in condemnation. They realized that their actions and behaviors were not in line with the law.

Understand, the Jewish nation was never known as a perfect religious example. They messed up continuously, but they were earmarked as the people of God. He loved them unconditionally.

Nehemiah could have used the opportunity to rebuke and condemn the people further. He could have belittled them and criticized them for their many failures. They certainly "deserved" it.

He didn't do that, however. Instead, he encouraged them to find their strength outside of themselves:

"Don't mourn or weep on such a day as this! For today is a sacred day before the Lord your God…Go and celebrate with a feast of rich foods and sweet drinks and share gifts of food with people who have nothing prepared. This is a sacred day before our Lord. Don't be dejected and sad, for the Joy of the Lord is your strength!" (Nehemiah 8: 9-10 NLT).

The children of Israel grieved because they could not do what was right in the eyes of God. They felt hopelessly separated from God.

Sound familiar? So many people are still looking for Joy when it has been hardwired inside of us all along. It has been going on for thousands of years.

But God is love, and love forgives a multitude of sins.

As that truth becomes evident to you and in you, your Joy will spill out of you–and you will feel compassion for others. It is a natural progression; the more you acknowledge how much He loves you, the more you want to pay it forward and love others. Jesus explained it this way:

"When you obey my commandments, you remain in my love, just as I obey my Father's commandments and remain in his love. I have told you these things so that you will be filled with my joy. Yes, your joy will overflow! This is my commandment: Love each other in the same way I have loved you" (John 15:10–12 NLT).

That is the final step in your dance to Joy–empowering others to experience God's love so that they will be filled with His Joy too. When you do that, your Joy will bubble over!

God Moments

Despite the blessings sharing your Joy with others can bring, this can be one of the most intimidating steps in reigniting your Joy. We all fear rejection and failure. It is inevitable with the enemy running loose in the world. Remember, God works through people, and it is His work through you. You do not have to take responsibility for success. Your job is to share your Joy with others, and God will do the rest–in His time and in His way.

This approach will lead you to experience so many gratifying "God Moments." God Moments are mysterious and cannot be explained but bring so much Joy because they validate that God is here and working in people's lives.

Seeing God moments in your life makes you want to pay it forward and share that Joy and incredible love with others. Here are a few God moments from my experience, some big, some small. All, surprisingly, wonderful!

Gwen

One of my best friends, Gwen, and I are both breast cancer survivors and have developed an amazing, empowering friendship. I have many God Stories related to Gwen, but the one I want to share is how God orchestrated our first meeting.

One night, I was on my way to a Bible study and stopped at a nearby deli to pick up some food. I met a lovely red-headed woman who was getting dinner too, and as women often do, we got to talking. I discovered she was also a breast cancer survivor. She invited me to join the local chapter of Project Pink'd, a breast cancer awareness organization. They do some beautiful things raising money to increase awareness, encourage and support women with breast cancer, and give back to the community.

No, that lovely redhead was not my Gwen. She led me to Project Pink'd, which I just embraced. I was asked to be one of the models for a fundraising calendar, and I attended the kickoff event with my grandson and family.

Gwen was a breast cancer survivor, and she and her husband attended the same fundraising event. He even donated his prized car to the cause.

No, Gwen and I didn't meet at that Project Pink'd fundraiser, although we were both there. We sometimes laugh at how we probably walked right by each other in the crowd of 600, never crossing paths through the entire event.

I had placed a Juice Plus advertisement in the fundraising program, and out of 600 attendees, one person saw my ad and gave me a call. That was Gwen.

We became good friends. Her husband died two years later, and, since I was a widow, we had a lot in common. I was in remission and supported Gwen through her painful cancer treatment while also mourning her husband's death. I so admired her strength and faith. I have seen her grow in Christ, recover from her cancer, and overcome so much pain. Her positive example has encouraged me to do the same. That stop at a deli and casual conversation with a stranger was the start of a God moment that landed me one of my very best friends.

Vito's Discovery

I have already shared many of my stories involving Vito, but there is one more that I consider a powerful God moment in our lives. When we first met, I prayed for guidance as to whether I should pursue a relationship or not. I was very guarded. Vito said in his thick Italian accent, "Whoa! You are a woman with boundaries. Ai Yi Yi!"

I kept feeling the hand of God in the glove, telling me to get to know this man. One night, we went out to dinner, and he raised doubts about where he would go after he died. I said to him, "What, you don't know you are going to heaven?" He replied, "No, nobody knows where they are going when they die."

It's like God pressed a big glove clad thumb in my back as if to say, "Stay close to this man. Share My love." I am so happy for that God moment, because although I miss Vito terribly, I know I will see him again in Heaven because he committed his life to Christ.

Family Brought Together

A miracle took place in our family after my husband's massive heart attack in 2006. On the day of Chuck's heart attack, our daughter called her brother, Chuck Jr., who lived in California to tell him about their dad. He arrived in Omaha the next day!

For me, the miracle was this: our son was scheduled to be away for several weeks the day Heather called. Instead, he was in Omaha, and spent three days in the hospital room with his dad. He was with us. If he had already left or didn't answer the phone, my husband would have died without ever seeing his son or experiencing our family being together at the end.

Juice Plus

The story of how I came to have a thriving Juice Plus business is the final God moment I want to share with you. I turned 60 in 2002. I felt miserable. I was always sick with colds and flu. I had problems with my teeth. My energy was non-existent. I didn't know what I needed to feel better.

I prayed, "Lord, I don't even want to talk to other people when I feel this bad. How am I going to serve You when I'm feeling so sick all the time? This is not how I want to live out my senior years. I want to serve You and make a difference. God, lead me to something. I don't know what it is, but this is not good. This is not good."

A while later, I attended a women's Bible study. As "luck" (read: the healing hand of God) would have it, my friend told me about a new nutritional product that had helped her through breast cancer by increasing her energy.

Typically, I would have responded to such an endorsement with much skepticism. I probably would have gotten away from my friend and the conversation as quickly as possible without being rude.

But that day, the Holy Spirit just jumped inside of me when I heard her. I listened to her attentively but went home without making any sort of commitment. She called me the next day and asked if I would be willing to listen to a cassette tape about Juice Plus, the nutritional product she talked about in Church. Even with my interest from the day before, I was very suspicious. It just was not in my nature to welcome what I considered schemes, even though she was a friend of mine. I was a skeptic.

However, I said a quick-arrow prayer asking, "God, should I do it?" And I said, "okay."

She sent me a cassette tape by snail mail. I listened and learned about Juice Plus' whole-food fruit and vegetable capsules. They are absorbed into the bloodstream immediately, giving you a mega dose of fruits and veggies with little waste. The research appeared sound, and I felt that gloved thumb poking me in the back again.

I listened to the tape, and it seemed like an answer to my prayer. I had asked God to lead me to something to feel better, and there was a possible answer.

I tried Juice Plus, and it was life-changing! I felt so much better that I wanted to share it with everybody. I decided to sign up to be a representative. What that meant was that I would share my experience with Juice Plus through a home-party. I followed my distributor's instructions and told people that I had something very exciting to share with them. My first party was great, I got seven new customers, and two others signed up to be representatives. Bam! I started a business, and I wasn't even expecting to do it. That was a God moment, leading me to better health and a new career. I lost 20 pounds that first year and ate salads, fruits, and vegetables and even lost my sweet tooth!

Through the years, I built a great team of Juice Plus reps that still today is like family to me. After Chuck passed in 2006, my team took care of the business while I grieved, and I had a purpose after I recovered. What a gift. When I was diagnosed with breast cancer in 2010, I was healthy through all the treatments. I never got sick. I was a little sluggish and tired after chemotherapy, but I never got ill, by God's grace. I was healed. I believe the whole food nutrition of Juice Plus helped my body stay healthy and build up a strong immunity and resistance to the poisons and toxins going into my body. The God moment that made me listen to my friend in church back in 2002 positively impacted my life over and over through the years.

It can be daunting to share the Joy of the Lord with other people. Never forget that God works through the small steps—a stranger in a deli, a "yes" to have dinner, or a nudge to keep listening when you'd prefer to do something else. Like the lovely red-headed stranger in the deli, you may never know how you fit into someone else's God moment. You are merely the glove, and He is the hand. You are not responsible for success. Share your Joy with others, and God will do the rest—in His time and in His way.

DAR GEIGER

CHAPTER 13
SHARE YOUR JOY

> *Do to others whatever you would like them to do to you. This is the essence of all that is taught in the law and the prophets. Matthew 7:12 NLT*

When I discovered how Juice Plus improved my health, I wanted to share it with everyone. I built a thriving business out of sharing my excitement. When something delights us, such as a movie, restaurant, or book, the first thing we want to do is share it. Sharing something special builds optimism and positive thinking–for you and the person with whom you share.

God wants us to share our Joy. People who habitually talk to people they are close to about the good things happening to them tend to feel happier and more satisfied with life. However, it goes further than "paying your good feelings forward." The Bible is clear that we should share the Joy of the Lord.

In fact, Jesus' directives on this have become what we know of as the Golden Rule: *"Do to others whatever you would like them to do to you" (Matthew 7:12 NLT).*

This charge can be a bit frightening. We often see Jesus' commands to mean we must become full-time missionaries or Bible scholars to share the Good News. One of the best ways to share your Joy is to simply share yourself.

Earlier in this book, I described how my friend and I share Joy every day by exchanging motivational quotes and scripture. That does not require a degree in theology to understand; it just takes a desire to encourage and be someone's buddy. You must share Joy with each other.

How can you share your Joy with others? I suggest you start by praying for God to provide you an opportunity. Pray for Him to place someone in your life who needs Joy. Share with others by living a godly life. Try not to do things that others might see as hypocritical by saying one thing but doing another. Show people that you care by spending time with them, serving them, and listening to them. You might not be able to answer every one of their questions, but they cannot deny the reality of what Christ has done in your life.

Share your Joy by living your Joy. Spend time with people. Have lunch or dinner with them. Attend Bible studies.

Or just have fun. I had lunch with a friend a while back, and we realized that we were dedicating a lot of our time to structured Bible studies. I don't deny the importance of being in the Word, but we became aware that we needed to play and laugh. God is calling us to do that.

Invite women over to play card games or for a movie marathon. A couple of months ago, I took dance lessons with six other women, which was so much fun!

My friend Gwen (who I introduced to you earlier in this section) and I have spent a lot more time together since Vito passed in 2018. We got together one day to cook a meal for a sick friend and had such a good time, and we started cooking together every Wednesday. One day I spontaneously suggested we video our cooking session. Gwen is more introverted than I am but was game to give it a try. We put some music on, which got us stirred up (pun intended), and we started hamming it up to the camera. It turned out so cute that we posted it on Facebook, which spread our Joy to our friends. We called our video (Wonderful World of Wacky Women Wednesday) at http://bit.ly/wackywedvideo because the "fun" title describes what our friendship is all about.

Since then, we have recorded several "Wacky Wednesday" videos together. They have brought a smile to many who have watched them. You are welcome to watch them too at https://www.facebook.com/dargeiger1 on Facebook. Making videos satisfy my craving to play and perform, and Gwen has learned to come out of her shell and blossom in a non-threatening way. It is a win-win-win for everyone, and not hard to do at all.

No Clowning Around

> *And let us consider how we may spur one another on toward love and good deeds, 25 not giving up meeting together, as some are in the habit of doing, but encouraging one another— and all the more as you see the Day approaching.*
> **Hebrews 10: 24-25 NIV**

Everybody has problems and challenges in life. When you invest in other people, you give your own issues to God and He takes care of them. Suddenly, your focus is not on your own misery. Your focus isn't on your pain because you're concentrating on other people, not yourself.

I mentioned I have always had the itch to perform. When I was growing up, I wanted to sing and dance on Broadway. As I matured, that dream faded as Chuck and I married and had children. Life's change of direction for me did not squelch my desire to perform.

In the 1980s, Chuck and I were both battling our demons, drinking too much, and making bad choices. We were at a party, drinking (of course), and I performed a dance for our friends that I thought was funny. Our friends thought it was funny. It fed my desire to perform. Man, I brought down the house.

Someone recorded the dance, and I showed it to my parents, thinking they would agree it was hilarious. Instead, they were appalled. They were so disappointed in me. Their reaction hurt me, but it also made me face how demoralizing the dance was. How condemning. I hadn't built a relationship with Jesus yet. Even then, however, He was nudging me away from my degrading behavior to other more empowering actions.

Not long after that, I was introduced to a professional clown named Bubblegum. She gave classes. I signed up for a session and learned how to be a clown. I called myself Scooter, and my clown character was a feisty little boy similar to Dennis the Menace. Bubblegum took her Clown school seriously; I had to pass all the training, and at the end, I took the Clown's Creed, which reads as follows:

"I believe I can best justify my existence by giving of myself as best I am able to, cheering others that they may be spurred by my actions to greater accomplishments of their own initiative."

At the time, I had no idea how much that Clown's Creed paralleled scripture, but looking back now, God was working through me even then. I just knew I was having fun, and Bubblegum was adorable. I was in a parade with her once. It took me three hours to apply my makeup, which threatened to melt off my face in the hot July sun!

After my invalidating attempt at that party to feed my desire to perform, Clown school was a bright and hopeful experience. I was able to spread such Joy at the parties and events at which I performed. I also worked with a minister visiting intellectually disabled adults. Seeing their smiles and hearing their laughter was food for the soul, mind, will, and emotions. Children at birthday parties would come up to me and tell me their secrets because I was one of them—I was Scooter! It was so heartwarming.

A smile has a ripple effect. However, my time as Scooter the Clown taught me that there is a difference between laughter and Joy. The two can certainly work together, but Joy is honest and real. Joy is helpful and encouraging. Spreading Joy has a purpose. I thank Jesus for prompting me after that unsettling experience at the party to do something really good.

When are you ready?

If you are wondering how to share your Joy with others, ask God. Pray, "God, what do you think would be the best thing for me to do today for others?" Listen to what God is saying and pray that the people you encounter during your day hear what God is saying to them.

Take a look around you. Do you feel the need to smile at someone or reach out and ask how they're doing? Do you want to tell somebody that you miss them and you would like to spend time with them? When is it time to start sharing your Joy? It is time when you feel God's nudge to give of yourself, to make a difference. I urge you to pay attention to that nudge.

Leap to share the Joy

I celebrated my 75th birthday by skydiving 18,000 feet out of a plane. I was terrified.

I have always secretly wanted to jump out of a plane. It is dangerous and exciting. It feeds my desire for experience.

Nevertheless, I was terrified.

My jump was tandem with a guide. God couldn't have been more present with me that day because my guide was an

Italian named Alberto that instantly reminded me of Vito. I felt comfortable and safe with him. I thought, God, you are so awesome! You've given me an Italian tandem rider! This couldn't get any better.

Yet, I was terrified.

When it was our turn to jump, we moved up to the opening in the plane. My foot, as if it had a will of its own, jammed against the side of the door, as if crying "nooooo!" It was an utterly reflexive response.

Because I was terrified.

Alberto calmly pushed my foot away from the door so that we could jump out. His strong arms surrounded me, and we leaped together out the door and into the sky. After the initial involuntary shriek, I looked around, and the view was amazing.

I saw the world differently. The ocean, the land, Cape Canaveral in the distance; I recognized them, but they looked different. My cheeks were flapping uncontrollably. I was delighted and inspired. We free-fell about eight seconds before Alberto signaled me to pull the cord for the parachute.

Suddenly, I was not terrified anymore. Once we leaped out of the plane, I had an overwhelming feeling of complete trust.

That is how God operates. Life is terrifying at times. It is so terrifying you want to jam your foot up against the wall and scream "no way!" Once you say okay and leap, that's when God comes through, wraps his arms around you and says, "I am with you! Let's leap forward in our relationship together!" Sharing His Joy is sometimes frightening. Surrender to the fear. Have courage. He will come through for you.

Start as an example

> **When God's people are in need, be ready to help them. Always be eager to practice hospitality.**
> **Romans 12:13**

Al-Anon and AA are spiritual programs where they teach you to change yourself and then add value to someone else's life. They are based on the principals of service. Buy someone a coffee. Give them a call. The entire 12-step program is based on the belief that, once you start seeing the light, then it is time to help someone else do the same. By doing so, you are helped even more. Serving others helps you.

Christians have a terrible reputation for being hypocrites. A hypocrite is someone who pretends to have virtues or God-based principles but does not demonstrate them when out in the real world. Or, as they define it in AA, someone whose talk doesn't match their walk. The party incident that led me to Clown School and my character of Scooter, the Clown stage, convicted me as a hypocrite. I blame it on alcohol, but my character did not match how I wanted to behave, whatever the cause. Thank God that he was working on my heart already, even though I hardly knew him at the time. He led me to Bubblegum the Clown, someone who was an excellent example to me of virtue and character.

The best and first way to empower others with Joy is to be a positive example. Never expect someone to do anything you are not already doing yourself. For example, how would someone react to you preaching about the sins of swearing if every other word out of your mouth is a curse word? You wouldn't have much validity. Your example speaks louder to your credibility and reliability than your comments ever will. People will judge you by how they see you live, not by how much you know or what you say.

What would Jesus do? He did not preach and condemn. He taught with love, examples, and parables. He taught the Golden Rule, as He lived it: Do unto others as you would have them do unto you.

God knows you will not always be the perfect example to others. You are human. Only God is perfect, but God does want you to model His love. The reality is that to some people, you might be the closest version of the Bible they will ever see. In other words, your example may make the difference between a person accepting Jesus or not. Don't let that freak you out, though. Your job is not to change people. God changes them. He is the hand; you are the glove.

Try sharing your Joy with someone else. Start with one other person. It is an investment. You will not see terrific returns every time that you share. I learned that lesson through sponsoring women in Al-Anon and AA. Some people will be thankless. Others won't want help. Still others drop out and give up. They would rather dodge the courage needed to make a change. God calls us to share our Joy regardless of whether we see results. Change happens in His time, not ours. He is the hand, and we are the glove.

So let's not get tired of doing what is good. At just the right time we will reap a harvest of blessing if we don't give up. Therefore, whenever we have the opportunity, we should do good to everyone—especially to those in the family of faith. Galatians 6: 9-10

FOR REFLECTION: SECTION 5
Empower Everyone

Questions:

- ♥ When you're in a tough spot emotionally, how do you comfort yourself?
- ♥ How do you feel about your feelings? Is it okay to feel the way you do?
- ♥ If you're lonely, what can you choose to do about it?
- ♥ Name a few things that make you feel happy.
- ♥ Are you willing to sacrifice for another?
- ♥ What might be the rewards?

CONCLUSION

Throughout this book, I have shared with you the fantastic future in store for you when you discover (or re-discover) Joy, as well as the heartbreak and anguish you may experience along the way.

The enemy knows that Joy comes from God and does not want you to find it. He is wily. He knows that God loves you and values you unconditionally. He knows God will help those who seek Him. So, the enemy works very hard to make people believe that they must depend on themselves; that God is not part of the picture - that Joy is not in your future.

TRUST – Try Relying Upon the Savior's Truth

"The B I B L E. That's the book for me. I stand alone on the Word of God, the B I B L E!" The Bible is God's love letter to us. There's a Bible in every hotel. I remember sitting in a hotel room when I was in a very dark place, with no Joy in my life. I was curious to find what God would show me, so I opened the Bible that I found in the desk drawer and began reading. I did not understand it all that night, but He sure did show me what He wanted me to see! That was the start of my journey back to Joy - by acknowledging and recognizing God's truth and that I was truly living in the wrong way, making bad choices, and that I needed to change.

Are you desperate and hurting? Are you trying to run on your own self-will? Are you at a point where you are crying, "I can't do this! I can't do this by myself. I need help." Jesus is there, waiting patiently and listening for you to call out to Him.

Your next action step is to talk to God humbly and ask Him for help. Ask Him to lead you to help. Ask Jesus to come dance with you. It's a prayer of the heart, a heart speaking to the Lord. And He will help you find Joy. He loves it when we ask for His help.

Maybe you're afraid, or you had bad experiences in the past. If you cannot reach out to God on your own, ask somebody to be with you as you ask for God's help. Go to a Bible-based church. Have the guts to say, "I'm hurting. I don't know how to pray. I'm scared." God knows your heart and will provide you the resources you need to find your Joy.

There's a song with lyrics that say, "If you can't trust God's hand, then trust his heart." Read His Book. When your heart is broken and contrite, His Word promises that He will help. God stands on His Word. God will show up whether you see Him and feel Him or not. He will heal your broken heart. That's a promise.

Suppose you choose to keep your Joy buried with your fear and pain. In that case, you can expect a very dark, dissatisfying, joyless, hopeless, despairing life. Today is the best time in your life to start your relationship with God. His promises, in the Bible, are absolute. You can depend and rely on Him to reveal those promises when you seek them.

Your life will change, and you will see hope and enlightenment. You will find the energy and your purpose for living. You will discover new relationships and renew old ones. Gratitude will fill your heart when you TRUST (Try Relying Upon the Savior's Truth).

FAITH – Fantastic Adventure In Trusting Him

Once you begin trusting in God's Word, a fantastic adventure awaits! Jesus wants to dance with you —to fill your life with Joy and delight. He is never too busy for you. Never. The scriptures are full of validation of how much He values you. He longs for you to live a life filled with goodness, Joy, and perseverance—a life of FAITH.

God will not force anything on you. Yes, He wants your heart, but He wants you to reach out for His hand and come to Him. He doesn't judge. His grace is sufficient. He wants you to turn to Him and say, "Please help me."

Does everyone hit rock bottom before finding the Lord? No. Some people grow up knowing about Christ, like Vito, who I introduced to you earlier in the book.

Vito thought he knew everything about God, but he didn't know Jesus Christ personally. He wasn't living a Fantastic

Adventure in Trusting Him (FAITH). He did not have God's Joy.

The Lord (working through me) stepped in, and Vito was born again! He told anyone who would listen, in his Italian voice, "I'm a newborn!"

Vito found his Joy by learning how to have a personal relationship with Jesus. He discovered just how easy it was to talk to Jesus and that Jesus would help him with whatever he was going through. He is dancing with Jesus today!

Maybe you grew up knowing about God but do not have a personal relationship with Him. It is never too late. He is waiting for you. Ask for forgiveness for trying to run your own life, and dance to Joy!

Expect challenges. You may find yourself doubting that any of this is true. Those are not thoughts planted by God but by the enemy. God is loving and encouraging. He wants you to rise to His purpose and plans for your life. He wants you to thrive.

G.P.S. – God Plans our Steps

We thrive by trusting in God's plans. He promises us we do not have to go it alone. God is our G.P.S.; He plans our steps. The Lord says, "For I know the plans I have for you, plans to prosper you and not to harm you, plans to give you hope and a future." (Jeremiah 29:11). If you doubt which way you should go, turn to your G.P.S., and know that God has no doubt. You can make a move forward, and He will back you up.

Developing a relationship with Him will bring you inexplicable Joy. It takes time to build relationships but investing in forming a connection with God and becoming aware of His love will give you the answers to your questions. The solutions are in the scriptures, but you must take the time to discover them.

BELIEVE – Blessed Every Day by the Lord's Increase of Empowerment for Victory and Energy

A life well-lived is one where you know your significance and can influence others to have a purpose and a reason for being. Everybody wants to know they have meaning. Everybody matters, and we must matter a lot because the enemy is continuously trying to tell us it's not true. Doubt seeps in, and that's when you need to reach out to a friend who can be supportive, pray with you, and guide you. You can be that friend to somebody. God works His stories through relationships with others.

Relationships are not just meaningful; they mean everything - your relationships with others and your relationship with God. He has so many promises to deliver to you. He loves everyone. Love Him back!

Be humble to the Lord. Humility does not mean thinking less of yourself to the point where you don't matter. Do not be shamed into thinking you are unworthy. Shame is not from God.

No, true humility is merely thinking of yourself less often. Learn about God's love for you. Then, share it with others, as God instructs: "Love one another as I have loved you"

(Matthew 7:12). Love Jesus. Love others. Love yourself. That's Joy. Joy and laughter are evidence of the hope we inspire in each other.

J.O.Y. – Jesus, Others, then Yourself

People everywhere are suffering. When they reach out for help, someone has to tell them about Jesus Christ. That's why God's Word says to "Go out there and help people, share the Gospel of Jesus Christ" (2 Corinthians 1:4). I used to pray that God would supply just one person a year for me to impact. I realize now that, with God's strength, I can help Him touch so many more. I am the glove; He is the hand.

I love to encourage and empower new and growing believers. We may be the only Bible people see. And there's a promise in God's Word; when we strive to be an example for Christ, His power is in us. Jesus said that "anyone who has faith in me will do what I have been doing. They will do even greater things than these because I'm going to the father." (John 14:12). I pray every day, "help me exemplify you, Lord, and *you* do the work *through* me." I am the glove; He is the hand.

I have shared throughout this book how God has changed my life and brought me Joy. He changes others, too. A friend felt crushed and broken-hearted recently because some of her family members were oppressing her Joy. I knew what was going on and saw the enemy at work.

God prompted me to call my friend and tell (not ask) her, "I'm taking you to lunch. Can you go Tuesday or Thursday?" Jesus told me to take command. She needed to

154

be loved on, and I knew it. That is how God works through us. It is that simple.

We had lunch at my home, and I asked her to pray about joining a Bible study. After our lunch, she told me, "Dar, you have no idea how much your invitation is *exactly* what I needed."

That's the Joy of the Lord. God worked through me because I was willing to take a simple action. Sometimes people become so paralyzed; they're hurting so badly that they cannot think straight or make decisions. That's when we have to feel the nudge and say, "I'm taking you to lunch." We are the glove; He is the hand.

God says, "Let all that you do be done in love." (1 Corinthians 16:14). When we do let him work through us, living a life of vitality is rewarding and energizing. Our life takes on meaning.

You are here to bring value to others, and it's not always a Joy ride. You will cry with hurting friends because you cannot fix what's wrong. But you can be there for them, pray for them, and support them. The Holy Spirit will give you the instructions. You can depend on Him to guide you. That's the value of having a personal relationship with Jesus. He is the hand, and you are the glove!

Remember, you have great value. You have the power to give another person a smile, a hug, or words of love. It does not have to be a big thing. People are hurting, and they want you to listen, without judging or trying to fix them. Just listen, and trust that God will work through you. You are the glove; he is the hand.

You don't have to work to change others. You don't have to spend a lot of effort changing yourself. That is the Holy Spirit's job. All you need to do is receive His love, acceptance, encouragement, and Joy. He does the rest of the work.

Faith is being sure of what you hope for and certain of things you cannot see (Hebrews 11:1). Faith brings Joy. Joy brings vitality, energy, and curiosity. You *can* find that treasure mentality.

My final wish for you is that you live a life full of vitality, knowing your true value in Christ and how much He loves you. He wants the best for you and your loved ones. My heart desires that you open that magic box to find the treasure that awaits. It's an invitation to the grand ball! God is waiting to dance with you for the rest of your life, here on earth, and when you join Him forever in heaven.

If you are just beginning to learn His promises, don't turn back now! The Joy you find on this earth is nothing compared to what is in store for you in heaven. Talk about Joy and laughter! Enjoy the promises of heaven. I know where I'm going, and I pray you'll be there too. We will be dancing with Jesus! No more sorrow and no more pain. All glory and dancing with Him! See you there!

ACKNOWLEDGMENTS

Writing a book at this time of my life was not on my radar...but apparently God had his plan in motion long before I was aware of the transformation that was taking place. He has nurtured, shaped, molded, broken, remolded, and transformed me in the most interesting ways that have made me who I am today.

Therefore, I want to acknowledge my Heavenly Father first. If it were not for Him, I believe I would not be here today.

Next, I want to extend gratitude for a wise kindred spirit, Dr. Rachel Smartt, who I feel was put into my life at the perfect time to prompt me to consider the idea of writing a book. She is not only wise, but relatable and fun, and has poured out her heart and experience to train and empower me to write my story.

I will always appreciate my publisher, Marty Dickinson, at ProduceMyBook.com who has the perfect answer for Type-A personalities like me, who would rather talk about life than sit down and write about it and do all the other required tasks.

And, finally, the original purpose for writing my story was to leave a legacy for my children, grandchildren, and future generations that they may know the hope to which God has called them.

ABOUT THE AUTHOR

Dar Geiger was born and raised in Chicago, and now resides in Omaha, Nebraska. Her closest friends prefer to call her Dar "fun" Geiger. She is a breast cancer thriver, and volunteers for Project Pink'd, a local breast cancer organization.

After years of running away from God, Dar chose to chase after him. Her vulnerability to share her journey is not only inspiring, but helps readers believe that it's possible to live their lives to the fullest.

Her intention is to spread energy, joy and stability to others in a confusing world that we've never seen before. Dar believes that God works in mysterious ways to bring blessings out of trials.

DAR GEIGER

ABOUT SNOWY RIDGE BOOKS

Being published and self-published book authors ourselves, we have experienced the same peaks and troughs of emotions and challenges as most authors.

We have developed a new way to develop non-fiction book content that completely removes the negative experiences associated with traditional writing.

While our books are published under the Snowy Ridge Books label, we provide training and support for our content development method through our sister website: ProduceMyBook.com

Produce My Book provides you with many benefits beyond traditional book publishing:

- Create your initial manuscript faster, usually within two weeks.
- Eliminate writer's block and enjoy producing content again!
- Reduce frustration by not having to type your manuscript from a blank page.
- Save money by not having to hire a writing coach or ghost writer.
- Increase content quality by producing more complete content than you would generate on your own.
- Get e-book AND printed books without having to pay up-front printing costs.
- Enjoy the process because you are working closely, one-on-one, with our staff from beginning to launch.

Go to ProduceMyBook.com to watch our free signature talk describing our non-fiction book development process in detail.

If you would not normally take the time to write a book, or have tried to write a book for years, here is your chance to share your expert method with the world!

Snowy Ridge Books
PO Box 441024
Aurora, CO 80044-1024
ProduceMyBook.com
crew@ProduceMyBook.com